GEORGE'S DAUGHTER

Carol Becker

I0518020

SPUYTEN DUYVIL
New York City

ISBN 978-1-963908-38-1
Library of Congress Control Number: 2024947104

"Carol Becker has written a tender, deeply nuanced portrayal of a father and daughter's evolving relationship, rich with love, betrayal, and the ruptures brought by shifting identities and a transforming New York City. Her poetic prose, suffused with details, romance and heartache, stayed with me long after reading."
—Ramin Bahrani, Oscar-nominated, writer-director, filmmaker

"After having written about attainable empowerment among women in mediating changes toward growth in *The Invisible Drama: Women and the Anxiety of Change*; grieving over the death of her beloved mother in *Losing Helen*; Carol Becker, once again, has resourced her "amor fati" to confront impending personal issues with her father in *George's Daughter*—her trilogy as it were. Suffused with compelling prose, emphatic clarity, and eventual compassion, her personal reconciliation through the arts and humanities as healing agents, mirrors our own."
—Phong H. Bui, Publisher, Artistic Director of The Brooklyn Rail, Rail Editions, and Rail Curatorial Projects

"This book is not just a beautifully written memoir. It's a story about the human condition. Neatly laid out sentences on pages jumble and leap with the complexities of life, love and loss. A reminder on the fallibility of relationships which traverse landscapes of memory and time, the book is also a journey into the most difficult and human of all possible actions, the act of forgiveness. Could there be a more poignant lesson for this troubled world"?
—Brad Evans, Director of the Centre for the Study of Violence, University of Bath

"*George's Daughter* is a journey of return—to Carol Becker's spirited childhood in an intricately drawn Jewish/Catholic family in immigrant Brooklyn and to a complicated yet beloved father. This tender and beautifully written memoir is a rare glimpse into what it means to come to terms with the mixture of love and anger, attachment and heartbreak that makes the ties between daughters and fathers unbreakable."
—Marianne Hirsch, Author of *The Generation of Postmemory: Writing and Visual Culture After the Holocaust*

For George and Helen and the roots that go deep

Contents

Nunc fluens facit tempus, nunc stans facit aete.

"The now that passes produces time,
the now that remains produces eternity."
—Boethius, *The Consolation of Philosophy*

Prologue:
The Old Neighborhood

After Mother Earth (Gaia) warns Zeus that his children could surpass him in wisdom and take his place as king of the gods and keeper of the law, he decides to kill them all. And when he learns that his first wife, Metis, is pregnant again, he decides to swallow her whole. Later, he suffers violent headaches that cause him to howl in pain. Desperate, he asks the smith god Hephaestus to crack open his skull with an ax. As his head splits in two, out pops Athena, "fully formed," dressed in armor as a warrior but personifying "wise counsel"—"an idea completely hatched," invulnerable and uniquely powerful, even among goddesses.

Although not an invincible goddess like Athena—nor a phenome about whom it could be said, "No mother gave her birth"—I certainly caused my father to suffer some violent headaches. There are those who would say that my actions prompted his near-fatal heart attack. Still, there is no question that I adored him and he me, and yet our life together was fraught.

My mother called my father Georgie, but I always called him George. I am not sure at what age that began, perhaps when I was five years old or younger. I do remember declaring something like: "George, we've known each other long enough. I am now only going to call you by your first name." It was not just that I was precocious, I was confident—in his affection, in his appreciation for my intelligence, in his love for our relationship as father and daughter but also as friends. We shared a great deal temperamentally— a New York sense of irony, an irreverence for convention, and a too-easy disappointment when people did not behave as we hoped they would.

The story of George and me, this story, is weighted with contradictions, polarizations, issues of gender, race, class, and identities (inherited and chosen), religious beliefs, pain, loss, betrayal and reconciliation. At the core is a drama about rupture, an undoing so painful that it almost destroyed us both. But only now, decades later, do I understand that it is also a story about forgiveness—him of me and me of him.

Our life together begins in Crown Heights, Brooklyn--a New York City neighborhood that, in the 1950s, was already cracking under the strain of its own history and the racialized politics and economic inequities of post–World War II urban development. The conundrum of my inherited Jewish/Catholic identity—a Russian Jewish father, a Polish Catholic mother—was only one aspect of the complexities that surrounded me. This dual identity, layered onto the heterogeneity of the neighborhood, dissolved all notion of absolutes, then and now. I would forever approach the world as "both/and," an intrinsic inclusivity that would shape how I understood my reality and reconciled the rest.

Whenever I need to reconstruct who I am, consider the essential matter out of which I am formed—how the molecules are configured, the cells organized, what gives me courage, makes me laugh, cry, rejoice, be generous or intolerant—I return to the ambiance of that Brooklyn neighborhood and to the memory of that time with my parents, family, neighbors, and friends who inhabited it with me. On those streets I learned to fear, to fight, to flirt, and to love. Although I now have a more objective knowledge of that place and time, its power to ground me does not live in a cerebral understanding of its sociology but rather in a childhood reverie that resides in the body, where its vividness has barely diminished.

While many of us who grew up in the boroughs of Brooklyn, Queens, Staten Island, and the Bronx in the 1950s recognize that these neighborhoods have transformed repeatedly since we inhabited them, they may still dominate our imaginations, not as they are now, but rather as they were then, our originary homes. Those who moved away as children or young adults soon learned that the cultural complexity inherent in these neighborhoods could never be replaced by suburban homes with baseboard heating, two-car garages, and contiguous squares of lawn. Sanitized, invented communities, where the appearance of each house was so homogeneous that it was easy to mistake one for another, never had the gravitas of those buildings that some families fled because the population was "changing," which euphemistically meant that a new group of residents of a different race or religious orientation had moved next door. Such lines around class, race, religion, or all of the above were being drawn at that time and New York City was beginning to feel less hospitable to everyone.

Writer Grace Paley, an inveterate New Yorker, well understood that those who once lived in such neighborhoods and who, during the "white exodus" of the late 1950s and early 1960s, moved their families to Long Island, Westchester, White Plains, or the Jersey suburbs, often referred to the site of their once familial home base as "the old neighborhood"—as did their children, who later visited the locations where their parents had been raised and their grandparents often still lived. The "old neighborhood" became a concept, a reference point of memory for an impoverished, ethnic past, whether Jewish, Italian, Irish, or Lithuanian. Like an American shtetl, the "old neighborhood" was a place from which families had fled long ago and which some hoped to forget and others chose to remember, not as it necessarily was, but as they imagined it had been.

In Paley's short story, "The Long-Distance Runner," Faith, the forty-two-year-old Jewish narrator, takes the IND train (later known as the BMT and then the D) to Brighton Beach where, in the 1950s, her father had bought shares in the Salty Breezes Beach Club and "still clears about $3.50 a year . . . which goes directly (by law) to the Children of Judea to cover their debt." Faith changes her clothes in the locker room and begins the long run to and through the "old neighborhood."

Faith, whose family had moved away from this place some time ago, had become a long-distance runner. "I was stout and in many ways inadequate to this desire," she says, but, nonetheless, she runs until she reaches her former building. Standing at its entrance, she is immediately surrounded by a large group of Black men." "I used to live here," she tells them and, like a Greek chorus they reply, "Oh yes . . . in the white old days. That time too bad to last." "But we loved it here," she retorts. "We never went to Flatbush Avenue or Times Square. We loved our block." The conversation soon degenerates and, frightened by what she perceives as a hostile undercurrent, she runs into the building, seeking refuge with a Black tenant, Mrs. Luddy, now living in Faith's childhood apartment.

Faith stays for months absorbed in the life of Mrs. Luddy, a single mother, and her family. She also tries to be useful by changing diapers, reading to the children in the evening and, for a time, assimilating into their lives— until they finally tire of her need to re-inhabit the past and throw her out.

Paley's story is a unique flight of fancy but not very different from states of mind I have inhabited while standing outside my former Crown Heights building on Albany Avenue and Montgomery Street, looking at our ground-floor apartment. At those times, I am only partially conscious that my former childhood home would now most likely no longer be occupied by Jewish or Italian tenants but rather by Black, Jamaican American,

West Indian American, and white residents—or perhaps by young Black, Brown, Asian, or white artists and entrepreneurs.

In Paley's story as well, the white Jewish world that once dominated Faith's building is long gone, and other cultures have become dominant. The violent history of Crown Heights and of many other Brooklyn neighborhoods attest to the fact that these transitions have not been easy. But it was there, then, in that place, that I learned how polarized and polarizing the world could be, there that I came to recognize and deeply mistrust racial and religious discrimination, and there that I learned to live in a truly heterogeneous, although fragile, society that could quickly have become explosive. Little could I have imagined that the ease and joy with which I had navigated such diverse populations later would become not only a great strength, but also the source of a cataclysmic break with my father.

I admire Paley's narrator for bringing on the weight of it: the degree to which we each have to absorb our own past to move into the future and, often reluctantly, accept change. History rolls over all of us, painfully: People we have known since our birth die, and we must construct our world without them, even as we desperately long to bring them back. Inevitably we want to set the play in motion again, rewind the film from beginning to end, adjust the script, only a bit perhaps, and briefly revel in the story, character, and textures of our early lives one more time.

After Faith returns home, she explains to her

incredulous sons where she has been: "A woman inside the steamy energy of middle age runs and runs. She finds the houses and streets where her childhood happened. She lives in them. She learns as though she was still a child what in the world is coming next."

But what is "coming next" after the child draws the adult back to their common point of origin— the place they each recognize as home—where the child first imagined the person she would become? Does the adult recognize the child? Does the child accept the adult? Can these parts of the self be reconciled? Or will the child always measure the dream of her potential unrealistically and unfavorably against the person she has become? This is the conundrum that the child may be running from and toward for the rest of her life.

Her journey begins here.

PART I:
TO INHABIT

Tell my story, begs the past, as if it was a prayer....

—Terrance Hayes, "For Brothers of the Dragon"

When those lucky American men, like my father, returned home alive from World War II, they and their families needed places to live. This period was the beginning of the baby boom in the United States and also the apex of a housing shortage that had started in the Great Depression of the 1930s, when new construction across the country had slowed to a halt. Small-town industry, which had accelerated during the war, was also now almost or fully shutting down. Many families looking for work were relocating to cities, including to New York and its boroughs. But there were no places to rent, and in some locations the situation was so serious that prefabricated homes known as Quonset huts became the norm.

From 1946 to 1952, Robert Moses and the New York City Housing Authority set up Quonset huts for returning veterans and other groups. An estimated two hundred thousand such structures were installed in Jackson Heights, Middle Village on Jamaica Bay, and in Corona, where the no-fee apartment community Lefrak City now stands, and in Idyllwild, which later became part of Idyllwild airport, renamed "JFK" for President John F. Kennedy in 1963. These corrugated metal dwellings, freezing in winter and stifling in summer, only emptied of residents in 1952. Some of these structures were relocated to other parts of

Queens and Long Island, and others were converted into garages and car washes. Few people can imagine that these inhospitable dwellings once housed what has been called the Greatest Generation and their families.

My parents were fortunate. Thanks to one of my father's three sisters, my aunt Harriet, who was already living at 424 Albany Avenue, Crown Heights, my parents found an apartment. When Harriet heard that a neighbor was moving out of the building, she asked that neighbor not to tell anyone about the move until she could check to see if her brother and sister-in-law still needed a place to live. When her neighbor finally did inform the landlord, my parents were first on the waiting list, which is how they acquired the one-bedroom, ground-floor apartment where I spent my childhood.

When you mention Crown Heights to those who lived in New York in the 1950s, they may make assumptions that are no longer necessarily true. Like most of Brooklyn at that time, Crown Heights was an insular, working class, middle- and upper-middle-class immigrant neighborhood: a mix of Eastern Europeans, Italians, Irish, Scandinavians, Blacks, and Orthodox, Reformed, and Lubavitcher Jews living together in good housing stock, not unlike the extremely diverse neighborhood along the large boulevard of the Grand Concourse in the Bronx. At that time, if one wanted to "eat out," stretch beyond a roast chicken cooked at home or a pastrami sandwich from the local deli, the only daring Crown Heights culinary experiences possible were a Chinese combination plate for $1.25, or a slice of kosher pizza for $.26. There also were no secular cultural institutions in Crown Heights, apart from the movie theater on Carroll Street—where the children's matinees on Saturday featured three Jerry Lewis/Dean Martin movies, alternating weekly with three horror movies and the ubiquitous ten cartoons.

If you extended the parameters of the neighborhood to include the area around Prospect Park, you then had the best of the borough: the Brooklyn Botanical Gardens, the Brooklyn Museum, the Brooklyn Children's Museum, and the Grand Army Plaza Library—all a good walk down Eastern Parkway from our apartment building. Some children, like myself, ventured forth to draw mummies at the Brooklyn Museum's free children's art classes on Saturdays. But if you never left the block, there was still plenty of cultural complexity to absorb.

The stately brownstones on President Street easily accommodated a professional class of doctors and lawyers who bought these properties and set up offices on the ground floor and lived with their families on the upper floors. Some very large houses and small mansions on Eastern Parkway also became Jewish temples or dental offices, like those of my orthodontist.

By 1957, fifty-two percent of the population of the neighborhood was Jewish, and there were thirty-five synagogues ranging from Reformed to Hasidic. In 1960, seventy-one percent of Crown Heights inhabitants were

Jewish and white, and the rest were Black. But by 1970, the population had shifted, and only twenty-seven percent of Crown Heights inhabitants were white, and most of these were Lubavitcher. Before the 1991 hostilities around race exploded and permeated all neighborhood relationships, the people living in this complex and diverse neighborhood seemed to get along. My first boyfriend, or "special friend who happened to be a boy" (other than my male cousins who lived in our building), was my fifth-grade classmate, Hubert Hunt. He was tall, thin, handsome, and Black. No one seemed to object to our friendship. He and his mother—who taught grade school—lived in a large brownstone on Carroll Street, around the corner from our building on Albany Avenue. I do not remember ever meeting his father. Because his home was so much larger than ours, our group of friends often met there to do our homework or play together after school.

Years later, when I was attending Winthrop Junior High School, I was introduced to the Congress of Racial Equality (CORE), and then the complexities of race in the neighborhood and in the country became much more prominent in my consciousness. I had a close friend at Winthrop named Emily, whose parents were actively involved in the Civil Rights Movement, which was not the case for anyone in either my Jewish or Catholic families. I think now that Emily's parents were probably artists, writers, beatniks, or all the above, although none of these categories existed for me at that time. Because of their influ-

ence, I began to read writers such as J. D. Salinger, Herman
Hesse, and the Beat poets—especially Allen Ginsburg—as
well as the philosophy of the Tao Teh Ching. Emily's parents took me with them to CORE meetings. Emily and I
were not the only young people in the room, but we were
the only young white people. I am sure the subtleties of
the conversations eluded us, but the fact that such meetings took place—people gathering to discuss difficult issues of race—settled deep into me. I remember picketing
Woolworth's department store in Brooklyn with Emily's
family because Blacks were not allowed to sit at Woolworth's lunch counters in the South. The protests in New
York City were in solidarity with four African American
students who were denied service at one of these lunch
counters in Greensboro, North Carolina, and then refused
to leave. I had only a vague notion of this event at the time,
but I did understand that one group had been discriminat-
ed against by another, so I joined the picket line outside
Woolworth's with Emily and her parents. Like everyone
else marching, I was carrying a sign. Mine must have read,
"Stop Jim Crow," because a man on the street, probably
noticing how young I was, shouted at me: "Do you even
know what Jim Crow means?" I doubt that I really did, but
I understood injustice and humiliation. Not being served
at a lunch counter in the United States in 1960 because of
one's race was just that—a grave humiliation and, to me at
this time, an incomprehensible violation. They took us all
to jail that day, just to unsettle us I think, because I can't

remember anyone being charged or spending the night. My father came to get me, but, remarkably, he was unfazed by the situation. Perhaps he already understood that I was outraged by injustice, and although not necessarily sympathetic to issues of US racism in general, as a Jewish man who served in WWII and fought against the Nazis, he must have understood what discrimination meant and where it could lead.

During the 1990s Crown Heights became infamous for the race conflicts and riots that occurred between Blacks and ultra-orthodox Jews. But race, racism, objectification of the other, and discriminatory practices had been present in Crown Heights even during the 1950s, although perhaps not yet as apparent to us as children. There already were many inherent conflicts between Lubavitcher Jews and reformed or secular Jews, between Lubavitchers and Blacks, and between secular Jews and Blacks. These tensions ultimately catalyzed the departure of less orthodox Jews—like my parents, aunts, uncles, and friends' families—from Crown Heights. Of these tensions, those that seemed most omnipresent and unsettling to the well-being of the neighborhood at that time were those between the Lubavitchers and everyone else. The Lubavitchers were often overtly hostile to those of different races and to other Jews outside their sect.

THE LUBAVITCHERS

Menachen Mendel Schneerson (the Seventh Rebbe of Chabad) came to Crown Heights in 1941 from the Russian town of Lubavitch. To escape persecution in the Soviet Union, he had first gone to Europe, but when the Nazis came to power, the Lubavitchers were compelled to leave for the United States. This religious community, one of many such sects within Judaism, grew enormously in the 1950s. At one point, there were ten thousand Lubavitchers living in Crown Heights. Theirs was a very insular community, a people apart, who lived in isolation for generations in Russia and in parts of Europe. In the 1950s, they structured their communities in Brooklyn in the same way, and they continue to do so today.

Less religious Jews, like my family and others in the neighborhood, resented the Lubavitchers for reminding them of the isolated shtetls of Europe that they or their families had escaped. For some, the Lubavitchers were an embarrassment because they refused to assimilate. The men dressed, and still dress, in long black coats and large fur-brimmed hats, even on the hottest days of summer. At that time, the women shaved their heads and wore badly fitting wigs and unfashionably long, loose skirts—as do some to this day.

To Rebbe Schneerson's credit, he started schools where women could study Torah, but men and women students were still segregated by gender. While the world of the 1950s and 1960s was becoming more progressive for women—women who, like my mother and aunts, had been in the work force their entire lives, including during the war effort, and now were returning to jobs because their children were older and in school—the lives of Lubavitcher women seemed traditional and fundamentalist. These women stayed home with their very large families (often ten or more children), at times proselytizing the teachings of their sect on the streets of the neighborhood. The older girls helped their mothers care for the younger children while the boys went to yeshiva—Hebrew day school—in large, rickety yellow school buses. Although many were our same age, these boys seemed like old men to us, dressed in black pants, white shirts, black jackets, and black felt hats, just as their fathers. They all had *payos* (side lock curls) around their faces, *yarmulkes* (skullcaps) on their heads, and *tzitzits* (silk fringes that men and boys wore attached to their *tallits*, shawls) hanging from their waists.

But perhaps what truly separated and also alienated my Russian Jewish family from these neighbors, and even from other Orthodox Jews (including my Jewish grandfather, who had wanted to be a rabbi and prided himself on his mastery of the Torah) was that the Lubavitchers looked down on other Jews. Whatever inclusiveness the Rebbe might have hoped to transmit, most Lubavitchers in our neighborhood believed, and acted as if, they alone were the Chosen People. To them, all other Jews—even those who had been persecuted in Europe and had escaped the Holocaust, had survived the camps, had lost entire families to the Nazis—were not considered real Jews. They, like everyone not in the Lubavitcher sect, were treated as heathens.

Many years later, when I was living in Chicago, I was introduced to a Lubavitcher rabbi through a male friend who was studying Torah with him and wanted me to meet his teacher and his teacher's wife—both of whom were Moroccan Jews who had studied at the Sorbonne. I was invited to a Shabbat dinner at their home, where the young couple lived with their six children. When I met the rabbi, I reached out to shake his hand, but he pulled back. Instead, he positioned his right hand across his heart and told me that he could not touch a woman who was not his wife. He asked for my Hebrew name, and, not wanting to explain that I was half Jewish and half Catholic, I offered my middle name, Dora. When the rabbi learned that I had lived in Crown Heights during the 1950s, he asked if I had ever met Rebbe Schneerson. "Met the Rebbe?" I said, incredulously. "Not only had I never met the Rebbe, I had never even seen the Rebbe." During all my years growing up in that neighborhood, I had never gotten to know a Lubavitcher man, woman, or child and certainly had no access to the Rebbe. The only encounter we had with our extremely religious neighbors was with Lubavitcher boys. We sold them cigarette butts, in small brown bags, a quarter a bag, retrieved from our parents' ashtrays.

Most adults I knew at that time believed that the

Lubavitchers had "taken over" the neighborhood, even though Lubavitchers had been living there since the 1940s. These same adults were equally unsettled by, and more fearful of, the many Black families now moving into Crown Heights. They worried about potential racial warfare. At that time, the population of Crown Heights was white, Black, and Hasidic—not yet also West Indian and Jamaican as today. The racism, or fear of otherness, was then still mostly manifested in passive-aggressive ways. If someone was selling a house and, for whatever reason, wanted to upset their neighbors, they sold it either to a Lubavitcher family, who, in celebration of the Sabbath, might dance and sing all night, or to a Black family, whose mere presence was thought to be a provocation to their white neighbors. The Lubavitchers even organized a vigilante group called the Maccabees to protect themselves and their homes from any potential violence. Men with long beards, wearing white button-down shirts and black pants, patrolled the neighborhood in old beat-up cars, chasing away with sticks and brooms anyone who they thought should not be in the area. This ad hoc group angered our Black neighbors, who were most often the victims of the group's aggressions.

More violent and protracted racial conflicts and riots erupted in Crown Heights in 1991, after a car in Rebbe Schneerson's motorcade hit and killed Gavin Cato, a young Guyanese American boy, on the Rabbi's return trip from the cemetery. Although there was no doubt that the collision was an accident, Rebbe Schneerson never made a statement or a visit to Gavin Cato's family or talked publicly to his own congregation about the importance of compassion and nonviolence. Any of these gestures might have helped assuage some of the tension in the besieged neighborhood. Instead, the situation devolved into total chaos when—in retaliation for Gavin Cato's accidental death—Yankel Rosenbaum, a young Australian Lubavitcher and a PhD candidate visiting Crown Heights, was stabbed and killed by Lemrick Nelson and a group of Black youth. The worst of the confrontations following Rosenbaum's murder occurred right under the windows of our former apartment on Albany Avenue and Montgomery Street. When I returned to "the old neighborhood" a year or more after these incidents took place, I was unnerved by the ubiquitous police presence. I wanted to show my then boyfriend and now husband Jack where I had grown up, and as our car pulled up to the building, officers came out of their parked vehicles to ask what we were "doing" in the neighborhood.

After the Rebbe died in 1994, Crown Heights became more racially divided. It grew into an even larger Lubavitcher enclave and a shrine to the late Rebbe, whose home at 770 Eastern Parkway is still preserved intact. Some Lubavitchers believe that Rebbe Schneerson will return as the Messiah, but on this speculation the Lubavitchers divide. There are not only those who refuse to believe that Rebbe Schneerson will have a second coming, but also those who are angered that fellow Jews would ever embrace such an apocalyptic world-view. Nonetheless, for many years after his death, a wide, white, plastic banner, attached to a tree with ropes, hung across the width of Montgomery Street, announced in black letters that, "The Rebbe is Coming. The Rebbe is Coming. The Rebbe is Coming."

424 ALBANY AVENUE

In my musings about my former neighborhood and building, I often try to recreate the space of my childhood. Unlike Faith, the character in Grace Paley's story, who finds another family living in her former home, in my imaginings our apartment, 1A, is empty of any new inhabitants and remains exactly as we left it. In this state of consciousness, I am still a child. I lie down on the yellow-, blue-, gray-, and red-speckled linoleum floor in the small foyer. I look up and "walk" across the ceiling, as I often did as a child, doubling the space of our miniscule one-bedroom apartment. Now upside down, I step across the doorjambs and touch each corner wall. Then, right side up again, I step into the living room, switch on the celadon porcelain chinoiserie lamp with the faded, fluted, cream-colored shade, and examine the objects on the mahogany table: the heavy, silver lighter with the delicately raised floral pattern around the base and the silver ashtray with the bright green felt pad that protects the metal from scratching the wood. And just as I am about to blissfully sink into the lime green, brocade-covered, high-backed armchair, the memory of a familiar, rancid, moldy smell stops me: a mixture of cat pee and garbage, seeping up from the damp basement.

Built in 1923, the red brick building at 424 Albany Avenue, a four-story walk-up with an interior courtyard, has a stone facade with the street address etched into the cornice. We, the many postwar children living there then, used the interior courtyard like a walkie-talkie, calling up and across its width to our friends on other floors whose windows faced the open space that separated one side of the building from the other. Because our apartment was just steps up from the lobby, I could easily walk out through our heavy, fireproof door to the baffled-glass window to the right of our apartment entrance. I was able to open that window high enough to sit sideways on the small ledge and shout across to my best friend, Hannah, whose fourth-floor kitchen windows faced the courtyard. Sad looking sumac trees, that barely survived the lack of direct sunlight and the moist black, clay-like soil, sparsely populated this wide courtyard. These trees never did flourish and surely did not bloom with those wine-colored, velvety, sculptural blossoms displayed by sumacs in more advantageous conditions. We yelled across those impoverished trees to arrange visits to friends' apartments or meetings in front of the building to set up games of stoopball, stickball, punchball and kickball or to agree on a time to walk to the schoolyard to play handball against the irregular cement walls.

Together we would round the corner to make wishes on a small fragment of white porcelain, with pink, inlaid flowers—once part of a plate or teacup—that had accidently embedded itself in the concrete when they built the small staircase leading up to this single-family house. We attributed magical powers to that splintered porcelain bit and summoned these when we needed help. We also gave names to things and situations using words and sounds whose meanings we did not understand but simply enjoyed shouting out: If you hit a sharp edge or a crack in the wall with your rubber ball and it ricocheted in unexpected directions, it was called a "Hindu." If you used your fisted knuckles to grind circles into someone's arm to cause pain, it was called a "Noogie." If you did the same thing to someone's thigh with an equally nasty intention, it was called a "Grivitz." If you grabbed someone else's Spalding (we said "Spaldeen")—a pink rubber ball that bounced extremely high and smelled like musty cherries when new—and threw the ball to another friend, forcing the owner, in a desperate attempt to retrieve the ball, to run back and forth between both tormenters, then one of the victors triumphantly yelled, "Salugi!" as the humiliated and frustrated owner usually dissolved in tears.

We were a tight pack of children, always together. At times, we roller-skated on the streets wearing heavy, metal-wheeled skates that we attached and tightened to our shoes with a "key." As the wheels grated against the granular concrete sidewalks, the noise was deafening. And when we fell, as we often did because the cracks in the uneven sidewalks upset our balance, we would scrape our knees and bleed all over our clothes. Such injuries took days to scab over often leaving a ridge of raised flesh as a scar.

There was a woman in a nearby building whose husband worked nights. We only became aware of their situation after we flew past her ground-floor apartment one day on noisy skates, unaware that her husband was trying to sleep. From her window, she screamed that we "lacked respect." After that, we tried to avoid her block, but sometimes we forgot and skated in front of her windows unintentionally. Then we had to double-down and skate even faster to avoid the pots of water she was preparing to throw at us. We never lacked respect, not at all. We understood what it meant to work nights and to have to sleep during the day—several of our parents did that—but we were kids in constant movement and often oblivious to the close proximity of our neighbors on these dense Brooklyn streets.

After dark, we would congregate in an apartment, usually mine, because my mother did not care if we jumped on the furniture or ruined the carpet. Material possessions were never particularly important to her. Many of my friends' mothers tried to protect their furniture with heavy plastic slipcovers on their couches and plastic runners over rugs.

Some even had plastic bonnets for their plastic flowers, but not my mother, who used to say, "One day when we move, I'll have real furniture," implying "then I'll care." In college I became close friends with a group of boys who had grown up in the Amalgamated Housing Projects in the Bronx; they told similar stories about their mothers trying desperately to save the furniture. My friend Bruce's parents were high school teachers who went to Europe for two weeks each summer. They would rope off the living room to protect their green-velour couch and chairs, probably their most cherished items, from their sons and their adolescent friends so that, while the parents were away, the boys would be reminded not go into those rooms and spill food and drinks on the furniture.

Our apartment was inescapably small. So hard to come by, it also was probably the rent my parents could afford at the time, thirty dollars a month. All the rooms fanned out from the small foyer. Single-child families like ours, customarily had only one bedroom. Those with more children sometimes had two, but not always. Our bedroom was only big enough for a double bed and a dresser. Next to that was a small bathroom with black-and-white hexagonal-shaped floor tiles that I still often see in buildings of the same vintage. There was one narrow window with baffled glass, a clunky white bathtub and sink, but no stand-alone shower. The galley kitchen had a built-in cupboard with glass doors for the dishes, a small refrigerator and stove, and a gray-speckled Formica table with chrome legs that was pressed against the wall, leaving only enough space for two metal chairs with yellow oilcloth seats. One was crammed next to the stove and the other abutted the small window with bars on its lower half that faced the street. My parents and I could not have eaten together at that table had we tried, unless one of us sat on the yellow step stool we kept under the sink. We could have all sat together at the larger table in the living/dining room, but seating was rarely an issue because we usually ate in shifts. My father often came home quite late, having already had a take-out dinner from a diner or Chinese restaurant near one of his stores. I usually ate in front of the television (once we had one) with my cousin Mark or another friend from the building, balancing our dinner plates on TV trays. My mother must have eaten alone in the kitchen or perhaps at the dining room table near us.

There was one closet in the foyer and one in the bedroom. I put everything that did not fit in my toy box (a large wooden chest in the foyer) under the double bed in the bedroom. When my mother complained to my Jewish grandmother, Esther, about my propensity for clutter, she said that my father had done the same thing: everything under the bed. My stuffed animals, however, slept on top of the bed, which was not my bed, although I did sometimes claim it when friends slept over and we shared it, while my parents slept on the convertible sofa in the living room. Most of the time, I was the one who slept on that dark-green brocade sofa bed that doubled as a couch. I removed the cushions and opened it each night by myself, just like the young girl on the TV ad for Castro Convertible Sofas. I identified with her, assuming that she also did not have a room of her own. Dressed in a light-blue nightgown and blue ballet slippers, with her hair pulled back in a ponytail and fashioned with a matching bow, she demonstrated how effortlessly she could open that bed, using only one hand. I sometimes tried to do the same, but if I moved too fast, I would scrape my leg against the gears of the heavy, metal folding mechanism on the side. Once, I dropped the frame on my toe, and eventually the nail turned black and fell off.

I never had a room of my own in Crown Heights. From the mid-1950s on, I shared this living room, my sleeping room, with the television. The first TV my father tried to bring home was stolen from the back of his station wagon before it reached our front door. But another soon appeared. This one had a magnifying glass attached to enlarge the 24-inch. screen. While my father worked and my mother slept, I watched movies late into the night— *Million Dollar Movie* (the same movie played all week). There was also *The Late Show* and *The Late Late Show*. I sometimes watched these movies again with my cousin or friends during the 7 p.m. screening and then watched them again alone at 11 p.m. My mother often took a bath before going to bed early, filling the apartment with the scent of lavender soap. She would kiss me goodnight, her face slippery with Pond's cold cream, before going off to the bedroom. I stayed up engrossed in movies like *Yankee Doodle Dandy* and *Casablanca* until my father came home hours later and talked to me about his day. I cannot remember anyone telling me to turn off the TV or to go to sleep, although I suspect they probably did.

At some point, my parents let me play in our only bedroom during the day—probably because it seemed unfair to them that I did not have a designated space to bring friends. Still, my only memory of discomfort because of our lack of space was on Sundays, when my father was not working and therefore was also at home. Then, with all three of us together, the apartment seemed impossibly claustrophobic. For most of my life, Sundays have continued to create a condition of unspecified anxiety.

It startles me still to imagine how my parents and I lived in such close proximity for my entire childhood. At that time, the size of our apartment did not signal anything to me about our financial situation. So many of my friends lived in equally tight quarters and I always knew that my parents felt grateful that they had an apartment at all. But I realize now that there was simply no place to *be* in that apartment—not for my parents and not for me, which explains why I still feel unsettled when there is no door to close behind me or space to retreat to. I have trouble breathing when I need to be alone but cannot be, or when people take up too much space—either physically or psychically. I am certain I felt this way as a child, but I could neither articulate such thoughts nor do anything to change the situation. Now, at such times, it is often best for me to stay in motion, or, if possible, to distract myself with a project.

I assume my parents felt equally uncomfortable, and perhaps even trapped in this situation because on Sundays we all were thrilled to head for Jones Beach, Riis Park, the Rockaways, or Sheepshead Bay, where we tried to catch small fish, we called "Killies," using pieces of clam for bait. Other times, we went with friends and neighbors for an early dinner at the fabulous Lundy's seafood restaurant on the bay. In the colder months, with my aunts along, we made excursions to Long Island to look at model homes that we never intended to buy, admiring the baseboard heating, which, unlike our old radiators that clanked and groaned, made no sound at all. Or we went to see movies in Manhattan, followed by dinner in Chinatown, like so many other Jewish families. We often met my parents' friends on Mott Street, at some undistinguished, florescent-lit restaurant with Formica tables that someone in the group had recently discovered, an out-of-the-way place with little charm but great food. The adults ordered dishes that seemed exotic to me at the time, like Moo Goo Gai Pan, and Moo Shoo Pork. But as a child, I usually ordered Chicken Chow Mein and candied kumquats for dessert. Because of my lack of food sophistication and adventurousness, the group jokingly called me "a peasant." Next, we always walked to Little Italy and Ferrara's for cannoli and then to the Village to look in shop windows on Eighth Street, admire the clunky but fashionable (to me) oxford brown, hand-made shoes at Fred Braun's, or visit the then abundant overstuffed bookstores signaling endless possibilities.

In spite of its space constrains, the building on Albany Avenue had great advantages for me. I was able to live as if I had an always present, extended family, consisting of a gang of children born after the war and parents who took responsibility for all of us. Mostly the same age, we children all attended PS 221 together, waiting for each other every morning to walk as a group the five blocks to school and waiting again at the end of the day to return home en masse. Apart from my first cousins, Roberta (Bobbie) and Eleanor, none of these children was actually a family member. My "cousin" Mark's family—Aunt Bea and Uncle Ben—were Greek Jews and somehow related to us. Bea's mother, Mrs. Goldstein, lived next door and was like another grandmother to me. My uncle Ben was a cab driver who owned his own cab and his own medallion, which was valuable property in those days. He worked constantly and we rarely saw him during the week— night or day. On Sundays, however, our two families often headed out with him in his Yellow Cab for our weekly adventures.

My cousins Bobbie and Eleanor were the daughters of my aunt Harriet and her husband, Uncle Joe, who worked as a movie projectionist. I often stayed with them when my parents went out at night. Later, when they moved away and we were still living on Albany Avenue, I packed a little bag and was deposited at their house for weekends in Valley Stream, Long Island. I always got lost there when I went out on my bike alone because every house looked the same to me. Of my father's three sisters, I was closest to my aunt Harriet, in part because she lived in our building, but also because she had a quick, irreverent wit. Unlike my Russian grandmother (her mother) and my own mother, both of whom were superb cooks, my aunt could not cook at all, yet she had no self-consciousness about it. Heating up "minute steaks" on the stove's grill for dinner with baked potatoes every night or putting fish sticks under the broiler was the extent of her culinary skills. I admired that she did not care to be a great homemaker. It did not diminish her self-worth nor my adoration for her independence from traditional expectations. My uncle and her children did tease her, but they also enjoyed the fact that she was oblivious to what other women considered an obligation to perform, whether they liked it or not.

The Harwin family, like Mark's family, was also vaguely related to us. There was Dottie, Arthur (who must have worked nights because we never saw him), and two handsome sons—Stevie, who was my age, and Brucie, who was older. Dottie's mother had her own apartment next to theirs. In the summers, without air conditioning, the air in all our apartments was thick with humidity and car pollution. On horrifically hot nights, the Harwins, like many others, would leave their door to the hallway open, trying to catch a cross-breeze from the courtyard windows. Dottie would sit naked on a brown leather recliner in front of the open door, watching television and eating dinner from a folding tray in front of her. More than her naked, corpulent body, it was probably her lack of inhibition that fascinated and terrified the neighborhood boys, sending them screaming and nervously laughing away from her door. When the evenings were intolerable, Dottie's mother would sleep outside in front of the building on a chaise lounge beach chair. It was the same type of red, green, and yellow woven plastic chair that we all took to Brighton Beach and Coney Island, but hers reclined completely like a bed. She slept in her housedress, brought a pillow from the apartment, and covered herself with a floral-patterned flat sheet.

Our building at 424 Albany Avenue had a depressing lobby covered in small, greasy yellow tiles. In the center of the space was a large, dark, mahogany table that smelled of furniture polish. The rest of the room reeked of Lysol that infected the air and made it hard to breathe. There were two heavy, wooden chairs on either end of this table that looked as if they were stolen from Dracula's dining room— high-backed with thick arms that tapered into lion claws at the base. I never saw anyone sit in them. We surely were not encouraged to do so, or to gather in that space.

I am not sure who maintained the lobby, probably Tony, the superintendent (Super) of the building, who might have moved a wet, dirty mop across the tiled floor from time to time. He surely did not do more. Tony was overweight and wore tattered, gray work clothes. Both he and his dog had a glass eye, or so it appeared to us, although perhaps they both had cataracts. His wife, Margaret, reminded us of Popeye's girlfriend, Olive Oyl. She wore oversized, torn, colorless dresses that hung loosely around her bony body, her gray hair pulled back in a ponytail. Whenever I see the famous Walker Evans photographs of tenant farmers, especially the one of a woman in a cotton, short-sleeve housedress standing alone on a rickety porch, looking vacantly into the distance, I think of Margaret, who also seemed depressed and malnourished.

Our apartment level was called the ground floor, not the first floor, although the floor above us was designated as the second floor. We were just a bit higher than street level, so there were no fire escapes outside our windows. I could have jumped out onto Albany Avenue with little consequence. When my friends and I had lunch at our house, pressured to eat too much of something we did not like and made to feel guilty about the "starving children in China," we would throw handfuls of spinach or broccoli out our window onto the plants below. But the Super and his family really did live at ground level. Their front windows—flush with the clay-like dirt—were hidden behind the hedges and the short, black, cast-iron fence that surrounded them, so their apartment received almost no daylight. I was only inside that small, damp space once to deliver our rent check, and the vertical stacks of clutter terrified me. It seemed as if those piles could easily come tumbling down, trapping us all, were even one item dislodged. Maybe Tony scavenged things from the basement—a place we hardly ever dared to enter.

The basement had a concrete floor and moldy stone walls. It was almost entirely dark and smelled of cats, garbage, and dirt. When it rained hard and the basement flooded, these combined odors seeped up into our apartment. On such days, sickened by the smell, I could not eat lunch at home and would ask for money to go to Joe's Delicatessen on the corner of Albany Avenue and Empire Boulevard, where, during the week, at the counter, Joe served Chicken Chow Mein over white rice and crunchy dried noodles.

That dismal underground basement haunted my friends and me. Because there was no security door, anyone easily could enter the building's open concrete stairs on the north side, where the garbage men picked up the trash cans. We often imagined that someone might be hiding or living in the basement's dark corners. When I went to dump our household trash, I ran out as quickly as I could. There were old-fashioned washing machines and dryers set up for the tenants, but I cannot remember anyone ever using them. Everyone I knew preferred to transport their laundry in small shopping carts to the storefront washing machines "down the hill." One day, as we were returning from school, police cars converged in front of the building. Soon they were pulling a man out of the basement. He was wearing off-white pajamas, wire-rimmed glasses, and slippers. We speculated that he had escaped from Kings County, the enormous, hospital and psychiatric facility, not far from Crown Heights.

The orbit of our universe also extended across the street to another hill, where Peck Memorial Hospital stood. We treated the land surrounding the hospital as a local park. When it snowed, we rode our sleds down its bumpy terrain. In warm weather, we brought out beach chairs and sat in front of the black wrought-iron fence facing Albany Avenue. The hospital was demolished in 2003, and this, to us, once-luxurious green space, was then filled with ugly, low temporary structures clad in beige metal siding. Today the site has become a yeshiva and is no longer a public space in which to play, sit, or roam.

Mrs. Goldstein

For most of my grade school life, right under Mrs. Goldstein's windows, adjacent to our own apartment windows, was a roughly spray-painted tag that read, "Steven Dicktenberg loves Carol Becker." It was the kind of thing children do to torment each other. Steven Dicktenberg was the cutest boy in my fourth-grade class. I doubt very much that he was "in love" with me, but the tagging remained a source of embarrassment to me for several years until rain and snow finally wore it away and I went on to Winthrop Junior High School. Steven, who lived in a different neighborhood by then, was enrolled in another school and was unknown to most of my new friends.

Mrs. Goldstein's husband had died some years before we moved into the building. She spent her days cooking, cleaning the apartment, and doing the wash for her unmarried daughter, Ruthie, who lived with her and worked in "The City." Even in those days, I was amazed that Mrs. Goldstein still used an old, heavy, cast-iron iron to remove the wrinkles from her daughter's clothes. She heated the iron on the gas burner, dipped her fingers into a glass of water, and sprinkled the water onto the clothes as she pressed the fabric hard with a methodical motion, alternating between smoothing out the wrinkles with her hand and with the hot iron. Some years later, when her handsome son, Eli, who had dark hair and a five o'clock shadow, fell in love with a blonde Catholic girl—a *shiksa*—he wanted to marry, she was able to accept his decision only because she loved my Catholic mother and knew us well.

Mrs. Goldstein was religious, more than others in our building, and she often took me with her to Yeshiva Reinus, a small, street level, orthodox *shul,* similar to those you might still find in Eastern Europe. We passed it each day on our way to school, and my friends and I went there for the High Holy Days. The classrooms, where the boys studied Hebrew and learned their *haftarahs*, were downstairs, below street level. There were wooden pews inside and no adornments on the exterior of the building. Each year, the congregation built a *sukkot* outdoors to celebrate the fall harvest holiday, the Feast of Tabernacles, but that structure too was extremely sparse, except for a few palm fronds. At times I went with Mrs. Goldstein to a much larger temple on Eastern Parkway. She was happy for the company and delighted that one of the children in the building was interested enough to attend services with her. This synagogue must have been a Reformed synagogue because it seemed very modern to me, almost church-like; there was no upstairs section designated for only women or downstairs section only for men. All were together. Mrs. Goldstein spoke little English, so it was difficult for her to explain why this experience was so unique. The Reformed temple also was more-stately than others I had seen. It had wide stone stairs at the entrance, with a gigantic, bronze menorah at the top, visible from the street. But to me the services lacked vitality. There was no bacchanalian dancing and very little Hebrew spoken or sung at all. It was difficult to lose oneself in time and space, as I had often been able to do during the more traditional services at Yeshiva Reines.

At night, when Mrs. Goldstein and I came home from temple, we always walked in the middle of the street, against traffic. In her mind this was much safer than walking on the sidewalk. "No one can pull you into the bushes if you stay out here," she said. I had no idea if people were actually waiting to attack us, but, still, whenever I am alone or nervous on an urban street at night, I think of Mrs. Goldstein and walk in the middle of the road, dodging cars—and whoever might be waiting to pounce on me.

The boys in the building, many my same age, had to learn their *haftarahs* to prepare for their Bar Mitzvahs. But they hated studying Hebrew, and truly disliked their teacher, who was tall, lanky, in crumpled, stained clothes, with a long, full beard. He always smelled of onions, which he probably ate raw, like my Russian grandfather. None of the boys wanted to be near him or to be in any other restricted situation at the end of the school day. So, the Hebrew class became anarchic, and the teacher was unable to control the students. The mother of one of the boys gave him chocolate milk and a banana as a snack each day. Evidently this did not sit well with him, because, I was told, he vomited them up almost every afternoon.

I was the only child in my building who cared about Hebrew—which was odd since I was also the only child in the building who was not completely Jewish. Because boys and girls were separated at Yeshiva Reines and girls at that synagogue were not allowed to study Hebrew, I convinced my Russian grandfather to teach me. He probably would have preferred to have his grandsons as his pupils, but he was stuck with me because only I wanted to learn. But after a time, I told my parents that I would prefer a real teacher, and they then arranged for a woman to come to the house to work with me. She was very small and

Eastern European with a heavy accent. She watched as I practiced writing the Hebrew alphabet in pencil in old-fashioned, small notebooks with blue covers and gold letters. I did not have an easy time writing the alphabet, and my penmanship was as sketchy in Hebrew as it was in English, but I nonetheless tried to learn as best I could. Each letter was a mystery unraveling before me and, once mastered, allowed me more access to the prayer books in the synagogue. Thus, I was able to recite the Kaddish in Hebrew for my Russian grandmother when she died, without relying on phonetics.

Because the boys tried to miss Hebrew school as often as they could, they needed notes from their parents to explain their absences. Of course, they could not ask their parents, who did not know they were skipping class, to write these notes, so they asked me. And because so many parents were immigrants whose English was minimal and whose handwriting in English was awkward and childlike, I was able to pull it off—until I got caught. For one of the boys, I had written, "Marc Orenberg had lumbago and could not attend Hebrew School yesterday." This note caught the attention of the Hebrew teacher, who said, "a boy his age could not have lumbago," (now known as lower back pain). So, Marc confessed that I was the scribe, and when I was asked if I had written it, I could not lie. I had gotten twenty-five cents for each of those small missives, and I also did the boys' Hebrew homework for a reasonable fee. Later, I had a bit of a side business practicing their *haftarahs* with them, making the boys repeat them to me again and again. But although I could read the words, I surely had no idea how they should be sung.

I was very close to Mrs. Goldstein's grandson, Mark—although my father would throw him out of our apartment at least once a night because, for some reason, Mark would punch me in the stomach or arm while we were watching television. Like many boys in the building, Mark had a lot of aggression and often got into fights coming home from school. There were many such brawls during our five-block walk from PS 221 to our apartment building. I often went ahead, carrying Mark's coat, which I salvaged after he would toss it carelessly onto the street. When his mother (my aunt Bea) asked where Mark was, I always told the truth: "He's fighting, but don't worry he's not bleeding."

On most days, at 5 p.m., Mark and I watched the television show *Sea Hunt*, starring Lloyd Bridges as a deep-sea diver who encounters alarming creatures in each episode—stingrays, great white sharks, and, of course, the ubiquitous barracuda. We tried never to miss an episode. Watching was a great adventure, especially for my cousin, who would likely have become a zoologist or oceanographer had he had the opportunity. Mark always dressed for our viewings. Lying on his stomach in his bathing suit, with flippers in the air and a snorkel on his head, he was ready for all encounters.

Our parents worked long hours. Mark's mother was a dental hygienist who traveled into Manhattan each day.

She was an attractive woman, and when her hair began to turn gray, she would come downstairs, once a month, to have my mother trim her hair and dye it coal black again. Many of our women neighbors—all in their forties and beginning to gray—did the same. Our house often smelled of chemicals: hair dye, peroxide, and the ammonia-laden mix used to process "permanents" that we all had to make our hair curly or our already curly hair more so. My mother, who worked as a hairdresser in Manhattan, was a stable force in the building, giving advice to these women about their children, their husbands, and their hair.

Mark's father, Ben, often brought home animal treasures from wild places like East Hampton, Long Island, where he drove passengers in his cab. Ben was a very sweet person, who recognized that his son needed something of nature in his life and tried to provide it, whenever he could. One year he found a snapping turtle in the Hamptons, having just dropped off a fare from the city. The turtle arrived at 424 Albany Avenue in a shoebox that had a big rock on top to keep it closed and little holes punched along the sides so the animal could breathe. My uncle put some water in the bathtub and lowered the box down until the turtle slid out. Most of the family was afraid of this reptile, but they still would throw bits of lettuce and apples into the tub each day to keep it alive. Mark watched him lovingly, and it seemed meaningful to him to have such a creature in his home. But with the turtle in the tub and no stand-alone shower in the apartment, Mark's entire family would have to come down to our house or go to Mrs. Goldstein's to bathe. After some weeks of this, the turtle disappeared. My aunt Bea had demanded that her husband drive the turtle back out to Long Island, probably in the same box in which he had arrived, and then release him on a back road. My aunt was mortified at not having a bathtub of her own.

This situation has always reminded me of *The Metamorphosis*, Franz Kafka's novella, in which an entire family is disoriented and then undone when the son, Gregor Samsa, awakens one morning transformed into a gigantic beetle and is unable to dress or go to work. The family is both afraid and embarrassed by Gregor's new condition, and they try to contain him and their shame by sealing off his room from the rest of the apartment. Because neither the family nor the maid will enter his space, they toss food to him from the doorway, as if Gregor were a wild creature who might harm them if they got too close. Eventually he dies of starvation, an apple lodged in his carapace. The snapping turtle also could never have survived domestic life at 424 Albany Avenue for very long.

Soon after the turtle fiasco, Mark and his family left Crown Heights and moved closer to Winthrop Junior High School. They bought a small white house with a built-in garage and a bit of a yard, but within months, my uncle Ben died of a heart attack. Driving a cab twelve hours a day in the heat of the summer finally caused his heart to fail. Everyone thought my aunt and cousin would nonetheless be financially secure—the taxi medallion was worth quite a sum in those days. But my father soon learned that, unbeknownst to his family or ours, Ben had been borrowing against that medallion for years. As it turned out, my uncle had been a serious gambler, and there was nothing left. The news was devastating to my aunt on many counts, not the least of which was that she had not known, nor even suspected, that this generous husband and adoring father had gambled away their inheritance. As close as we all were, practically living communally in each other's homes, not even my father, who knew the gambling world quite well, had suspected Ben's addiction.

The Erratics

In Ireland they call large boulders that balance precariously on the ridges of cliffs "erratics." These enormous rocks, so visually different than others in the landscape—larger and more dominant—were carried great distances by glacial ice and miraculously perched in unexpected locations. In geology, an erratic is defined as any material that is "not native to the immediate locale" but has been transported from elsewhere. I think now of the many inhabitants of our Crown Heights building as such.

It is one of the oddities of childhood to accept, but not necessarily understand, the eccentricities that we encounter in adults and even in other children and yet to find in those people with unique personality traits or deviances of mind something dramatic—sometimes visual, cinematic, and deeply troubling, but always memorable. My childhood was filled with such people and their confusing, painful, and often inexplicable behavior. That they all landed in this one place can be attributed to the post–World War II housing shortage but also, more accurately, to the nightmares caused by the Nazi project to annihilate all Jews and many others and the devastating effects on those who miraculously survived and found their way to the United States but never truly recovered from the trauma.

We all knew about the concentration camps, but of course, as children, we had no real idea of the magnitude of what had occurred, why it had occurred, or what the experience of surviving such a catastrophe might do to someone. I personally had no understanding then, and now truly only a bit more, of how such unspeakable events as the witnessing of genocide and fearing for one's life every day could rip apart a human psyche, such that it may never repair. As philosopher Ludwig Wittgenstein wrote in the *Tractatus*, "That of which we cannot speak, we must pass over in silence." In our building, and I am sure in many others, there was a suffocating cacophony of Holocaust silence, which nonetheless dominated the conscious and unconscious minds of many in our midst. It affected even those of us who had not yet been born at the time and also those who had lived in the United States throughout the period, relatively unscathed.

Some neighbors had faded blue concentration camp numbers branded on their inner forearms, above the wrist. I now understand that these markings meant that these people all had been in Auschwitz. Their children were our friends. Yet, as omnipresent as the Holocaust experience was in our daily lives, we were offered no explanation of how such a thing could have happened, why it was not stopped, and what rationale was used to defend it.

While other children throughout the country were dreaming about Donald Duck, Mickey Mouse, and other benign cartoon creatures, in my neighborhood we were obsessed with Hitler, Himmler, Göring, and Goebbels. We understood that these Nazi leaders had killed millions of Jews. We understood they were evil. But because their actions were inexplicable and because we were also powerless to erase these figures from our consciousness, we could do nothing other than transform them into fools. And so, without really understanding why, we children sang these songs:

(To the tune of the march "Stars and Stripes Forever")

Göring had only one big ball. Goebbels had two but they were small. Himmler had something similar, and Hitler had no balls at all. . . .

(To the tune of "Whistle While You Work,"
from the Disney film *Snow White*)

Whistle while you work.
Hitler is a jerk.
Mussolini broke his peenie
and now it doesn't work.

Each year, on Yahrzeit, the Jewish anniversary marking family deaths, some families lit so many slow-burning candles, set in glasses on the ledge of enamel kitchen sinks, that at night, from the courtyard of the apartment building, their kitchens appeared ablaze. A single family might be remembering thirty or more lost relatives with candles that burned for twenty-four hours.

We did not know that there were homes in America without such historical trauma. We did not understand that it *was* trauma. We watched shows about American families, like *Father Knows Best*, and wondered aloud about a place where no one had an accent and everyone seemed to live in the present and not the past. Was their world truly free of such weight? When did those families mourn the dead?

There were always new tenants moving into the building whom we referred to as the "refugees." Many did not speak English, and we did not know where they had come from or why they had arrived in New York. One night, when water started dripping from the living room ceiling of our apartment, my father declared that it was because the "refugees" upstairs were washing their floors by pouring buckets of water out onto them and then mopping it up. "That's what they do," he said. "That's how they wash their floors." But how would he know what they did? And who were "they?" Perhaps these "refugees" were the new people I had seen coming into and out of the building that day. Perhaps he was right, and this was how they washed their floors—or perhaps the water leaking from the ceiling was simply caused by a broken pipe.

"Refugees" was the designation given to people new to the neighborhood, easy to mock and to blame. But in Brooklyn at that time, everyone was an immigrant, a child of an immigrant, or a refugee fleeing an impossible situation. Everyone was from somewhere else: my friend's German/Jewish parents, who barely spoke English; the Italian shoemaker who listened to opera all day on the radio; the Polish baker who made twisted dough cookies with powdered sugar called *kruschicki*; the Jewish baker who made *hamantaschen*, buttery pastries filled with prune or raspberry preserves and shaped like little hats. All these were immigrants, some had been refugees, and none spoke much English. They had just enough words to negotiate basic business. Still my Russian/Jewish grandfather loved to call those new to the United States "greenhorns." It made him—he who thought you needed a passport to go to Pennsylvania—feel righteous and American.

I knew some of the neighbors well; others were just part of the daily experience of our building. They often make cameo appearances in my memory. There were also people around me whose physical and psychological problems were probably unrelated to the Holocaust, but whose actions were equally inexplicable, eccentric, or often painful to us. As a result, we often laughed at things we should not have found funny. But we were witnessing an array of troubled, troubling, obsessive, neurotic, and destructive behaviors, and we had no language for any of it, and no cures. Some of my friends had learning disabilities or other impediments that limited their ability to comprehend, interact with, or even survive the New York public school system. We all observed exhibitionism and eating disorders, but the adults did not analyze such behavior—they had no tools to do so. In their world view, people were as they were, did as they did. If they knew about the existence of psychiatrists, therapists, and counselors, they would not think to consult them nor would they have known how to access them. There was freedom in this collective obliviousness for some, and tragedy in it for others. Because we did not really discuss the cause of these behaviors, someone might say that an uncle, cousin, or neighbor who was aggressive or inappropriate simply had something "off" about them or had a few "loose bolts." Older and perhaps somewhat senile people were said to have "lost their marbles." Even if a person was obsessive compulsive or phobic, *meshuga*, or "nuts," was the only explanation offered. These expressions certainly did not suggest a diagnosis, strategy, or cure. No one I knew was dangerous to others, although some were destructive to themselves.

There were those who lived lonely, isolated lives, unable to interact with anyone inside the building or with the larger world outside. They were the lost ones. I came to understand that a life could fail, and a person could end up desperately alone. I also observed how hard parents worked so that their children would have everything they needed. We were their hope, but, perhaps luckily, we did not understand the magnitude of their projection. My father often said, "Everything I do, I do for you." This statement made me so uncomfortable that I challenged him about it. I could not bear to think that his own life did not matter to him, that only mine was important. "But you and mother also need food, clothing, and a place to live," I would say. "It's not just for me that you work so hard." "No," he would say emphatically, "It's all for you." There would be no further conversation.

Friends, Strangers, Strangeness

My closest friend in the building was Hannah Kaufman, whose family lived above the Harwins on the fourth floor. Her Jewish parents, Greta and Josef, had met in a Displaced Persons camp in Germany after the war. While there, Greta had broken her wrist, which had never been properly set, and so forever was bent at the joint— her palm flat and her fingers outstretched, as if she were waiting to receive a serving tray. She almost never left the apartment—perhaps because of this deformity or because her extra body weight made it difficult for her to go up and down the four flights of stairs (there was no elevator) or because of all the painful events that had occurred prior to her arrival in Brooklyn. Greta was a very sweet person who was always kind to me. She had freckles, like her children, and seemed very happy with her husband, who worked for Garay Belts. I only ever saw her in housedresses and with her hair pulled away from her face, except when Hannah and I graduated from sixth grade and Hannah's parents came to graduation. Greta looked lovely that day in a yellow summer dress and hat. That's when she met my father, George, for the first time and told me that she thought he looked like the television newscaster Chet Huntley. Greta's sister, Genie, like movie stars of the time, wore deep red lipstick to exaggerate the shape of her lips. She came most days to do the family shopping and then carried heavy bags of groceries up the four flights of stairs, often with the help of Hannah's brother Max, who was brilliant in science and mathematics and who we all assumed would become an engineer. But, alas, and not surprisingly, given the traumas of his family, Max suffered from many psychological problems and never did fulfill these expectations.

The Kaufmans' apartment, like those of other friends in the building, smelled of what we called "kosher soap." This soap had an unmistakably disinfectant-like odor and came in large, thick, milky-white bricks with a somewhat faded band of blue dye embedded around its girth. I always associated this smell with the kitchens of our displaced Jewish neighbors until I encountered it again in Prague in 1989, while renting a room in a woman's house at a time when the City of Prague had few hotels. Such soap, I now understand, was an Eastern European product, first manufactured by Israel Rokeach of Kovno, Lithuania, in the 1800s and later brought to the United States. It had been "certified" kosher because it was made of coconut oil rather than animal fat and always left a thick, murky film on plates and glasses. Its smell so sickened me that I never could eat anything when this soap was nearby—neither at Hannah's apartment nor in Prague decades later.

Hannah and I often worked on projects together. I was always busy running for school officer positions in those days—president of the General Organization (GO) and class president. Hannah was my campaign manager, which meant she helped make the posters that we hung at school to publicize my various platforms. She was talented at executing ideas visually. She drew and printed well—skills I did not have. And she was always willing to help promote my career as a school leader. She was selfless in ways I knew I was not.

Instead, I was the child others followed, always chosen to run things, not because I was smarter than my classmates or even as smart, I often was just more decisive about what I thought we should do. My mother used to say that

I was "bossy," as if I coerced others into doing what they might otherwise not have chosen to do themselves. But I disagreed. I was assertive and I also knew my limitations, so I became adept at managing situations by asking others to do what they did well and I could not do at all—a strategy I still employ when trying to accomplish things today.

All the girls in my fifth-grade class, for example, had to make a cooking apron, and if we failed, we would not be promoted to sixth grade (or so they said). Although my mother was incredibly talented at such things, having helped make all her family's clothes out of flour sacks and recycled fabric for her entire childhood, I never learned to sew well and had little interest in acquiring such skills. I therefore struggled to complete this assignment. My apron was a mess. The stitches were too large and irregular, and my hands had soiled the fabric. The teacher must have been horrified when she saw my extremely inadequate creation, but she simply asked me, "What do you plan to do when you grow up?" In those days, I was quite certain that I wanted to be a veterinarian and proudly told her this. She then asked, "And what will you do after you have operated on an animal? How will you sew it back up?" I took a breath, looked out into the room, and pointed to my friend Susan Peck in the back row. "I will hire her," I said. "She sews better than anyone else in our class." I was not trying to act smart or funny—I was just practical. Even at that age I understood that one need not be good at all things. There were always others who would be expert at what I could not or would not do. But there was also my mother's ongoing critique that I was simply "not good with my hands." She, who grew up extremely poor on a farm in Pennsylvania, could fix, sew, or crochet anything, without a pattern and without assistance. She understood that, like my father, I was limited on the physical plane: we two were quintessential urbanites with few practical skills and not much interest in learning them.

My family once invited Hannah to spend a weekend with us in Deal, New Jersey, visiting my parent's friends Irving and Rose Block. Hannah had been raised in a strictly kosher home and surely had never had milk with meat or experienced too great a variety of food. So perhaps she had mixed foods she was unaccustomed to eating together or simply had some sort of stomach virus, but on the way home she was sick, and we had to stop on the highway several times so she could vomit. My mother asked her to sit in the back seat with her and to put her head on my mother's lap.

Because I had no brothers and sisters, I had never had to share my mother with another child in such an intimate way—so the image remains in my consciousness. I can still conjure the feelings of jealousy that this aroused in me. I must have been a possessive child, but I had few opportunities to experience myself in this way, and so I found these feelings humiliating. I also felt shame because Hannah's life was more stressful than mine. Her family struggled financially, and there was a palpable sadness in her home. Unlike me, she never left the block in the summer. Her aunt, who was already living in the United States during the war, was the only relative who had survived the Holocaust. It pained me that I would deny Hannah anything, even if only in my thoughts. Aware that my mother was just being kind to my friend, I was nonetheless threatened. It was the first time that I was able to observe myself as both irrational and inappropriate, but nonetheless unable to control my response. I was also able to observe how such anxiety could be manifesting internally, even while no one else was aware of it—an invisible drama. I learned how lonely such emotional states could be.

Single children, "only children," are at a disadvantage in this respect. We do not gain practice in negotiating emotions, such as sibling rivalry or jealousy. Nor do we know how to justify these feelings to ourselves when they do occur. Because "only children" are with adults so much of the time, they often forget that they are children, and so the bar to behave well, even the internal bar, is very high. The fact that I was not more mature at this moment brought me shame—shame I could not discuss with anyone and had few tools to process. To this day, I tend to take the bad behavior directed at me by others far too seriously. I am equally hard on myself when my responses, even those that go unexpressed publicly, are less than elevated. Siblings might compete with each other, but children without siblings compete with themselves. In that type of competition, there never can be enough success.

In a fourth-floor apartment near Hannah's, a middle-aged woman lived alone. This was rare at that time because "single women" in Brooklyn tended to live with their families. Angelina, appeared to have no family, and although she must have gone out to shop for food, we never saw her on the street talking with anyone. She was extremely thin with long, gray hair pulled into a bun at her neck. When we were out trick-or-treating on Halloween, we dared each other to ring her doorbell. And then we double-dared each other to stand in front of the door when she opened it. We would not have entered the apartment to get our treats, and we surely never ate anything she gave us, usually apples. We were not so much afraid that she was insane as we were certain that her apartment was a locus for alien creatures. Once, when I was standing far outside the open door among a cluster of other children peering around each other to see inside, Angelina pointed back into the living room and whispered to us conspiratorially, "They were here again last night," and, after a long pause, added, "They left watermelon pits on the carpet." It was just enough to send us screaming through the corridor and careening down the marble stairs.

She scared us with her imaginings, and we scared ourselves even more as we embellished them with our own. There was so much to fear from the past, the present, and the future. Ours was the era when nightly news reports were filled with tales of alien UFO "sightings." We actually did believe that space aliens might be coming to abscond with us to unknown planets and that new forms of enslavement were being devised, very much in line with what we were told was the totalitarian effects of communism. There was a popular film about a giant carrot-shaped, one-eyed alien hiding in a cave in the Nevada desert waiting to take over the world. There was *Invasion of the Body Snatchers* (citizens are slowly replaced by alien imposters) and *War of the Worlds* (a small town is attacked by Martians). By day, we had the Nazis of the past and the present-day repercussions of their perverse, horrifying behavior. And by night, we were surrounded by images of atomic radiation (another human terror unleashed in World War II) that had distorted nature and may have catalyzed the birth of mutated creatures, grown out of scale, that could no longer be controlled. There were endless filmic creations to validate this hypothesis and fill our imaginations: *Godzilla: King of the Monsters*, *Creature from the Black Lagoon*, and others more disturbing and bizarre, such as *Fiend without a Face* (giant brain-shaped creatures proliferate, spinal cords attached), and *Them!* (innocuous ants grow massive and destructive). In *The Killer Shrews*, voracious animals multiply and, having eaten everything else on an isolated island, turn to humans, who escape by rolling down to the sea in wooden barrels—the crunching of bones as the credits scroll alerted us that not everyone had made it on board the waiting ship.

On the other side of the building three stories up, lived Morris, who was probably in his forties. He always wore a shabby corduroy sports jacket and a gray, woven-straw hat with a small multicolored, pheasant feather on its black band—a style that you can still buy from most New York street vendors. None of us was ever able to peer into his apartment to see if he lived alone or with others. He told us that he was a "private eye." Different women, unknown to any of us, came in and out of his apartment several times a day—not something we were accustomed to in our building. So, we thought perhaps these women were somehow related to the cases he was trying to solve. I am sure our parents had other explanations.

Close to Morris lived my friend Helene and her parents. Helene ate so little that I think of her now as "the hunger artist." She told her mother, Ruthie—and anyone else who asked—that she once had swallowed a chicken bone, which had lodged in her throat and now made it difficult for her to swallow. Several doctors had been consulted, but none ever had found the bone. Helene was very petite and, of course, anorexically thin. Her parents also were tiny, as were many Jewish people of their generation. Some older women shop owners on Kingston Avenue were so small that they could not see over their counters without standing on a footstool. When we were in their stores, we often had to lean over to find them if we wanted to pay for something.

I had a book (which I still have) called *People of the*

World in Pictures. It is a thick, heavy, large-format volume, bound in a dark-brown leather cover with gold, flourished lettering. Inside are 1950s-era photos from *National Geographic* magazine, black-and-white and sepia-toned portraits of people from Lapland, the Congo, the Amazon, New Zealand, Zanzibar, and other locations—photographed in the straight-on portrait style popular at the time. And, as was true of these types of photographic projects, only Black and Brown people appeared naked or semi-naked. All representations revealed a colonial mentality, but we did not understand any of this at that time. We found some of the images curious and mesmerizing: Sami men wearing animal skins and riding reindeer. We experienced others as disturbing, depicting a cultural approach to the physical body we had yet to encounter: African women with extended earlobes, South American indigenous tribes with body piercings and Maori men and women with tattoos covering their entire bodies. If I wanted to terrify Helene (which I apparently sometimes did), I simply opened the book to any page and thrust it in front of her. Whether she looked at the photos or not, the very gesture would propel her into flight, screaming, almost falling over herself as she leapt up two marble steps at a time, back to her apartment. For me these images represented worlds I did not know and people I had never seen and could not have imagined. I reveled in the differences in culture they presented and in the idea of a world whose complexity seemed infinite. That book marked the beginning of wanderlust—my desire to visit every continent and to see as much of humanity as I could. But for Helene, the images had the opposite effect. They made her want to retreat to her apartment, forever.

My mother told a story about Helene's parents, Al and Ruthie, that, in her mind, explained Helene's extreme skittishness. My mother, Al, and Ruthie were together in our kitchen when a very small mouse ran across the floor. My mother did not move at all. But Al, who was a slight man, screamed and pulled himself up onto the thin ledge that ran around the cupboard. Ruthie leapt out of the room entirely. My mother was incredulous. "How can you be afraid of a little mouse?" she asked. "That mouse is more afraid of you." My mother had admirable equanimity. It took quite a bit to scare her. She had grown up under difficult circumstances—ten children in the family and a father killed in the Pennsylvania coal mines. The family had to pull together. She knew farm life and the creatures that came with it. She certainly was not afraid of a mouse, and she did not have tolerance for those who were.

Years later, an incident in Chicago reminded me of Helene's extreme fearfulness. I was living in a building owned by Robert Stoltenberg, a maker of violins and cellos, and his wife, Julie, who told me that she was phobic about whales. I had recently come from Southern California, where, over several winters, I had watched whales migrating to Mexico. I also had just finished graduate school and my PhD dissertation on Edgar Allen

Poe and Herman Melville (and, of course focused on *Moby Dick*). So, it was inevitable that Julie and I would talk about whales— her great fear of them and my fascination with them. She recounted that as a child, she had owned a hardbound edition of *Moby Dick* that had small, black-inked woodcut images of different kinds of whales on the upper right corner of each page. Wanting to read the novel without confronting the terrifying images, she closed her eyes as she meticulously folded each corner, sometimes losing several sentences from the top of the page in the process. I noted that she was lucky to live in the Midwest where she would never accidentally encounter any whales.

One day, an inexplicable event occurred: unbeknownst to Julie, the large, early twentieth-century armoire in her bedroom tipped over onto the bed. When she came into the room, she at first thought a whale had beached on the shore of her white bedspread. Terrified, she ran up the stairs to find me in my apartment. We went back down together and, with much effort, were able to right the armoire against the wall. As an adult, I was now more aware of my own irrational fears, and had grown compassionate to those of others. But unfortunately, I had not been so as a child.

Cyrano

My time on the farm with my mother and her family in Hastings, Pennsylvania, had made me something of a "country girl, living in the city," as my Uncle Jakie liked to say. He was right about this. I was surely at home in an urban environment, but I loved wildness, and during those early years in Hastings, I had become somewhat fearless when in proximity to animals. I learned to recognize when an animal was playful, or angry, unhinged and dangerous.

On the farm we had many cats (those that survived the weasels). Thus, it seemed quite normal to me to have a cat in Brooklyn, although in those days, no one we knew in the city had cats—Cocker Spaniels maybe, small turtles in bowls with plastic palm trees, parakeets definitely (although these often succumbed to fumes when people painted their apartments), but no cats. I had a habit of literally picking up "alley cats"—big tomcats bruised from battle, thick in body with stubby hair, dirty nails, and pug faces, smelling of garbage. Small as I was and as awkward as it must have been for me to carry these tough, squirming creatures, they, to their credit, never scratched me. I tried to make them pets, but they did not want to be domesticated, so instead I would bring food outside to them, although they never seemed terribly hungry. My own cat was named Cyrano, after the character of Cyrano de Bergerac whom I first encountered in a 1950s television production of Edmond Rostand's 1897 play. She was dirty, city white. When I received a *mezuzah* as a Purim prize, I put it around her neck to protect her, until someone in the building complained to my mother that it was insulting to Jewish people to do so.

We kept a small screen in the kitchen window that slid horizontally and could be left open so Cyrano could jump in and out at will. Once when my mother and I were visiting my grandmother in Pennsylvania—and my father was away, running the auction room in Point Pleasant, New Jersey—my aunt Bea was in charge of feeding my cat. She felt sorry for this creature that had to stay alone, so she brought Cyrano up to her apartment on the fourth floor. The cat must have spotted an open window in the living room because she jumped right out. Perhaps she confused her location with our ground-floor apartment. Or, more likely, she was just desperate to be free. But, on the way down, she was probably quite surprised to realize how high up she had been. My aunt told me later that she "just couldn't look." She was certain that the cat would be splattered on the sidewalk. "How would I ever tell Carol that Cyrano [which she pronounced with a Yiddish accent] was dead?" In fact, as is the case with cats, Cyrano landed on her feet and walked away.

Eventually, other cats began to follow Cyrano through that open window screen and into our apartment—leaping up the stone facade, onto the ledge, and into our kitchen. My father, a city guy with little love for animals, was mortified to find strange, dirty cats in the kitchen eating Cyrano's food. Soon after, Cyrano was taken "to the country." Where that white cat came from originally, I am not certain, and where she ended up is also a mystery. Perhaps she went the way of the small rabbits that arrived on my Easter birthdays. We always kept these bunnies for a time, but when they grew big, they were taken to a "farm in New Jersey." It certainly made sense to me, one who felt confined in the city, that animals needed space as they grew.

Perhaps all these animals actually did end up in the Catskills in upstate New York, where one of my mother's brothers, my uncle Butch, lived and ran a small chinchilla farm. Visiting there one summer, I was attacked by my cousin Patricia's otherwise docile Collie while I was swinging on a tire tied to a rope, flung over the branch of an enormous elm. Something about the rhythm of the motion must have set the dog off because it leapt onto me and ripped into my thigh. A doctor had to cauterize the deep wound, but luckily, I was spared the painful round of rabies shots, the normal protocol in those days when you did not know if the dog had been vaccinated, which, luckily, this dog had been. I still have the scar. But even though my cousin and I protested and cried hysterically, my uncle shot that dog. In his unsentimental country mind, a dog that would attack a child was a sick dog. And I had not been the first.

In my childhood, the presence of the war, the eccentricities and oddness of the apartment building, the claustrophobic feeling of living life in such close proximity to others was balanced by time spent in the natural world. For this I am grateful to my mother and her family. Summers in Pennsylvania provided a sense of freedom the city never could. To the city I owe my quick reflexes, developed as I tried to make sense of the neighborhood around me; to the county I owe my spiritual self—my calmness, my love of beauty, solitude, and order. Without this balance, the intensity of urban life would have consumed me long ago. In nature, violent as it can be, I have always found everything I have needed to reconstitute myself. "What I love is near at hand/Always, in earth and air," writes Theodore Roethke in "The Far Field." This back and forth between country and city was so much a part of my early life that I replicate it to this day.

When I first came to California as a graduate student, I lived by the ocean but then moved inland to an even wilder environment of rattlesnakes, cougars, and coyotes on a thousand acres in the Anza Borrega desert, east of San Diego. I also spent years going back and forth from San Diego to a cabin in Montana where I had a wolf/coyote/Husky-mix dog named Pisces—the great animal love of my life. During all my years in Chicago, I spent a great deal of time on the shores of Lake Michigan. Even now, while I am again living in New York, I return often to that lake, a great natural force that transforms itself daily. And when I am not there, I am walking in the Conservatory Gardens of Central Park or swimming in the Aegean, Ionian or Cretan Seas.

LEAVING CROWN HEIGHTS

During my childhood, our building at 424 Albany Avenue was walking distance from the now demolished Ebbets Field on Bedford Avenue near Empire Boulevard, once home to the Brooklyn Dodgers. The children in our building were devout Dodger fans, and we spent afternoons trading bubble-gum cards with pictures of our favorite players. But there was one boy in our group who rooted for the New York Giants. He wore a Giants baseball cap most days, which horrified the other children in the building. His father often took him to the Polo Grounds in Harlem to see the Giants play, and because we were loyal to our team, we ostracized him. One simply did not go against the Dodgers or their fans without consequence. But our cruel behavior made him pull away from us. He dropped out of school and out of our lives completely, and it was rumored that he became a gambler and a card shark.

Brooklyn was a village in those days and had several newspapers of its own. These publications—and the Dodgers—were our most prized possessions. We barely related to other New York boroughs, or they to us, and, for the most part, we surely did not champion their teams. And so, as many have written before me, when the Dodgers left Brooklyn in 1957, it was a betrayal of trust of such enormous magnitude that I for one stopped caring about professional sports, forever. What had once felt almost like a religion had been desanctified. It made no sense to us that the Dodgers would leave their hometown. How could they? Why would they? It was inconceivable that our beloved team would abandon Brooklyn for a new stadium, more money, or a chance to have more fans. It was even more incomprehensible that they would move to Los Angeles—a place about which we knew nothing. They might as well have left for Mars.

We did not understand the extent to which Brooklyn was transforming. The racial makeup of the neighborhood had shifted, and many white people, fearful of these changes, were not as eager to come to Crown Heights for games as they once had been. Many Dodger fans had moved out of the area entirely, and there was no parking at the stadium, which had been built in 1913. By the 1950s, Ebbets Field was in great need of repair. Also, everyone now owned televisions; people could watch games at home for free. As a result, the stadium's box office revenue had been suffering for a time. The Dodgers surely had their reasons for going. But we were too close to it— too young, too naive, too myopic and too romantic—to ever understand the lure of money and the West Coast.

Brooklyn was not the same after the Dodgers left. Its diverse, working-class, ethnic population was tied to that team of incredible players, some of whom, like Jackie Robinson, defied the rules and integrated baseball for all time. The Brooklyn Dodgers, with their once powerful local identity, had made us proud and then broke our hearts.

"White flight," as it has been called, accelerated by the mass adoption of cars and the subsequent development of suburbia, became a contagion in the later 1950s and early 1960s. And so, my neighborhood, like many others, changed. Some of my aunts and uncles moved to Long Island. Hannah's family, once on the list for the Ebbets Field Apartments, grew tired of waiting for the building's completion and left for Queens. Other friends relocated to Staten Island. My parents never understood the appeal of the suburbs, and my father hated to drive. So, they would never have chosen a long commute from the city. But by 1960 my parents began to talk about wanting me to attend a "good" high school, by which I now understand they meant one that was not predominantly Black. And so, we too finally left the neighborhood and moved to East Flatbush, close to Midwood High School, with Brooklyn College right across the street. We barely knew the area at all, but my father's sister, Julia, lived nearby. This move away from Crown Heights also catapulted me out of my extended family and social class and into a more homogeneous world—one that was predominantly white, educated, professional, and middle class. At the time, I only partially understood the enormous psychic disruption these changes would create.

PART II:
TO INHERIT

In the well-known biblical parable of the Prodigal Son, a man gives his two sons equal inheritance. One remains close to home to care for his father. The other defies the will of the father, goes forth, experiences life beyond the family, squanders his inheritance, and returns many years later, knowledgeable about the world but impoverished. Nonetheless, all is forgiven, and the father asks that a lamb be slaughtered to celebrate his returning son; the son who never left home receives no such honor.

But what if the story were instead about a daughter who defies the will of the patriarch, ventures out into the world without her father's consent, and then hopes to return to share all she has learned, would she be accepted back into the fold? Would the father rejoice, offering up a fatted lamb to celebrate her unexpected return? Or might he slam the proverbial door in her face?

HELEN

After courting for ten years, my Russian Jewish father and my Polish Catholic mother finally married. Their ambivalence to formalizing a life together was, in part, due to fear of being ostracized by their families for marrying outside their religions. As a result, my mother was thirty-nine when I was born. At that time, it was unusual to have a first child at such an age. In the linguistic conventions of the day, she used to say that she had had me "late." She had hoped to have many children, to mirror her own large family, but there were gynecological complications that kept this from happening. After "a surgical procedure," she was able to conceive me but could have no more children. Thus, I remained an "only child," the youngest among my New York Jewish cousins, who were all five to ten years older. As such, I was a greatly anticipated and then feted child.

As my mother told it, although in extremely vague terms, mine had not been an easy birth—neither for her nor for me. My Polish grandmother and my mother understood a great deal about home remedies. They could make herbal poultices and brews of all sorts that healed and helped, but they did not understand Western medicine and they approached it with a mixture of fear, reverence, confusion, and dread. So, my mother did not ask her doctor too many questions and, as a result, could never accurately describe what had occurred, but from the information she did offer, I was able to deduce that I was trapped in the birth canal for a dangerously long time (which, if true, might explain why I so easily feel claustrophobic). She said that the delivering doctor had alerted my father that either my mother or I might not make it through the birth. According to her, my father's response was that if a choice had to be made, the doctor should save my mother. I never knew whether her recollection of this traumatic event was accurate or if, during the delirium of labor and anesthesia, she simply had imagined this conversation. I have always thought that it was a story she did not need to recount to me. But whether the narrative was accurate or not, I surely never consciously blamed my father for making such a choice. Still, this narrative embedded itself in my psyche, perhaps offering, more than anything, insight into my mother's need to prove her importance to my father, superior to mine. Although I never doubted my mother's love for me, her remarks were often hurtful. Whether she was conscious of this propensity to compete with me and at times diminish me, I never knew.

Although I am convinced that my parents had a great romance, I am equally certain that my birth triangulated, or simply transformed, their connection to each other. Perhaps my mother was simply jealous of my father's adoration for me or of the opportunities my life later offered me, that hers had not, such as education. I do know that our shared love for George was a deep bond between us, but he and I were only part of her story.

EVANTHES

For many years before I was born and for some time while we lived in Crown Heights, my mother worked as a hairdresser on 42nd Street and Broadway at a location we always referred to by its Greek owner's last name: Evanthes. This salon was my mother's place of employment when she first arrived in New York City from Hastings, Pennsylvania, and continued to be for most of her working life. During the war, she took a hiatus and, like many other women of her generation, supported the war effort. When I was born and in grade school, she also stopped working at Evanthes, but she returned during my junior high school, high school, and college years.

When I was older and my mother was still working, I often climbed the four flights of stairs up to the salon to visit her. I went as often as I could because I knew she loved to tell her coworkers about my grades and my ambitions. She also simply enjoyed showing me off to her clients and especially to her boss, Paul Evanthes. The stairwell always smelled of ammonia and hair dye—an acrid but familiar odor.

Housed in a turn-of-the-twentieth-century office building, Evanthes was not a beauty salon as we think of such today—it was not luxurious, spa-like, fashionable, or well lit. Rather, it was a simple complex, consisting of serviceable offices that had been converted for a new purpose. One might have expected to see a cigarette-smoking private eye slouching over his desk in the adjacent suite. Each office entrance had a beveled glass door. Etched onto the salon's was the actual name of the business, "Originals by Paul." I could hear the chatter and clatter in their always busy "offices" as I approached the entrance. Theirs was a series of small rooms paneled in dark, varnished wood. Each cubicle had a brown, well-padded, and heavy-metal-framed leather barber's chair placed in front of a large mirror set within a marble-patterned Formica counter. Whereas the hallway was dimly lit, these spaces were glaringly, unflatteringly bright.

When my mother arrived in New York in 1925, she was sixteen and right off the farm. She used to say, "I didn't know how to do a damn thing then except sew, cook, can, bake bread, build fences, plant a garden, milk cows, and drive a tractor—nothing useful for city life." As the second oldest of eight children, she left school after fifth grade to help her mother take care of her brothers and sisters. Later, when the family needed cash, she headed for New York City, as did many others from her mining town. She had a friend from Hastings who was already living there. This friend was dating a Greek guy who had a brother, and that brother was Paul Evanthes. He was starting a business and he was hiring.

The hairdressers at Evanthes gave scalp treatments to men and women, but mostly to men, who were losing their hair. In my mother's first meeting with Paul, he explained, "Many people who come up to our place have dandruff, itchy scalp, a feeling that something is crawling in their hair. Scalp treatments can be very helpful. All you need to do, Helen, is use the ultraviolet wand. Then, after that, we'll put on the salve." It was easy. The hairdresser simply moved a clear glass tube, encasing a filament of pulsating ultraviolet light, in circles around the heads of the many bald and balding men and the few women with thinning hair who came for "treatments." Paul Evanthes believed that this fluttering light could increase circulation and encourage hair growth. The wand made a nasty, sputtering vibration that resonated in the glass, like the sound of a mosquito zapper. Paul was onto something back then. Stimulating the scalp can help promote growth, but my father was not convinced and called the whole operation "voodoo."

When my mother began at Evanthes, the salon had ten "girls" working "the wand," and three men who applied the salve. The first person my mother treated left her a $20 tip. That was more than her salary of $18 a week. Soon she was making $100 to $200 a day in tips—and there were plenty of extras. Broadway theater directors who came for treatments gave her free tickets to all "the best shows." Business owners from the garment district invited her to their factories to get fitted for clothes when they were "cutting a new line." She was thin then, with a slim waist and large breasts, and, as photos attest, she looked glamorous in these clothes. Soon she had a new wardrobe: cashmere coats with fur collars and matching fur-lined muffs, beaded opera jackets, fitted faille suits, satin undergarments, alligator shoes, velvet hats with "fascinator" veils and pheasant feathers tucked into the side bands, and $200 dresses that cost her $29.95. When my cousin Eleanor, then a child, saw her for the first time—tall, in a fabulous white hat and dress—she thought my mother was a "movie star." Who else would have such clothes and wear them with such confidence?

Evanthes also made wigs for those clients with

thinning hair and dyed the hair of Broadway performers. The location was perfect: the offices were in the Theatre District, and many dancers, singers, and other performers "came up to their place," especially if the casting call for the day required more blondes, brunettes, or redheads. When these "show people" were working in Los Angeles, they told their colleagues, "If you go to New York, you've got to get a scalp treatment at Paul Evanthes. And be sure to ask for Helen." My mother became so popular that Paul told her, "You're better known than the best hooker on Broadway." When he was about to hire another young woman, whose name was also Helen, he informed the new person, "We will call you Marie, so no one gets confused."

"Marie" was Italian and "a big girl," as my mother used to say. She had a husky voice and beautiful white skin, wore deep red lipstick, and her black hair in a "pageboy," straight cropped to her ears with bangs. When they met, Marie was the same age as my mother. They soon became best friends and remained so for their entire lives.

Marie's mother had abandoned her and her brother when the two of them were young. Her father, like other single parents at the time who had to work and had no one to care for the children, placed Marie and her brother in St. Joseph's Home, an orphanage upstate in Peekskill, New York, until he could figure out how to manage. But St. Joseph's, which was run by Roman Catholic nuns, was a tough place. Each child was paid twelve cents a day to clean the orphanage. Marie hated the work, but she hated the nuns more. On the day her father finally came to take her and her brother home, Marie was washing the marble floors. Another girl whispered to her, "Your dad's here to take you with him, for good." Marie kicked her bucket of water down the stairs, made an obscene gesture at the nuns, and ran to her father. When telling this part of the story, my mother always said, "That was okay for Marie. She was leaving. But you know those nuns made some other poor girl clean up the mess." Marie was fifteen when her mother reappeared. She asked Marie, who was then working in a factory, to move in with her. Soon her mother's boyfriend noticed that Marie had very few clothes and took her out to buy more. Her mother became jealous and threw Marie out. So, Marie appeared at Evanthes, looking for a job. Marie and my mother, who were both living on their own in the city, decided to share an apartment.

According to my mother, Marie soon hooked up with a "a mobster boyfriend," named Sal. He worried about two young women riding the subway alone at night, so he began sending his car and driver to pick them up from work, often taking them to one of his nightclubs for dinner. No one dared tell Marie that he was married, not even his brothers, who worked at these clubs. One day, surprisingly, the mobster's wife called Marie at Evanthes and said, "Beware of Sal. He's crazy, possessive, and he'll never let you go." The next day Marie told the boyfriend that she wanted to date other guys and was breaking off the relationship. "Let's not talk about it now," he said calmly.

"We'll go for a ride in the country and discuss it then." Somewhere in the woods of Long Island, he pulled the car over and put a gun to Marie's head. She did not flinch. "Go ahead Sal. Shoot me," she said. "Helen knows I'm out with you." They drove back to the city. He walked her up to her apartment, sat at the kitchen table, and leaned his head down over his folded hands. Marie then got a butcher's knife from a kitchen drawer and slashed him across his wrists. "Don't you ever, ever, threaten me again," she said. But for all her bravado, it took many years to actually free herself from that man. In the late 1950s, when Marie had her own small beauty shop in Williamsburg, Brooklyn, she got a call from a priest, who asked if she would come visit her former boyfriend in the hospital. "Sal's dying and he wants your forgiveness." Marie held Sal's hand while he whispered that he was sorry, very sorry. He said he knew that he "had ruined her life" but, he "loved her too much and could never let her go." After he died, Marie met Coco, a Cuban exile, who wanted her to marry him and move to Spain, but she would never leave New York. Turning her head from side to side with her eyes closed, my mother often said, "It's a shame Marie never married or had a family of her own. She lost her best years to that mobster."

HELEN AND GEORGE

When my father, George, first appeared in my mother's life, she was sharing an apartment with her friend Vivien. George was a pal of Vivien's boyfriend John. Because my mother loved to dance, she often accompanied Vivien and John to ballrooms around the city. John could never understand why my mother didn't have a date every night. One evening, he decided to invite "gorgeous George"—that's what they called my father in those days, an appellation that started in high school—so he could meet my mother. That night, George and John were coming back from a speakeasy, and George was uncharacteristically drunk. John kept trying to prop him up, but, as in a slapstick routine, George kept sliding down the wall. They sobered him up with coffee, and he then told my mother and Vivien that his name was George Cunningham. I am sure he had invented that surname so that my Catholic mother would not know that he was Jewish, although she probably suspected that this was not his real name.

George adored my mother from the start. He would have married her right away were he not worried about what his family might think of this glamorous *shiksa* and of what her family might think of this Jewish gambler. He also probably knew that a negative reception from his family would have hurt my mother. But his reticence to take her home to meet his parents only made my mother worry that a marriage with him would never work. Her family was central to her life, and she did not want to be ostracized by his. It surprises me now to think that my father was so reluctant to risk his family's rejection. He was always so irreverent of authority. Concerned that there was no future with him, my mother kept trying to break off the relationship. At times, George would wait outside her apartment and follow her on dates with other men. He would sit next to her in movie theaters, no matter what guy she was out with that night. Because he had a sweet tooth, he then would buy candy to share with them both and end up eating it all himself.

Their on-and-off courtship and complicated love affair went on for ten years, from 1928 until 1938—until, one day, George took my mother for a car ride with their close friends, Charlie and Ruthie. After driving for some time, my mother finally asked, "Where are we going?" Ruthie spoke up from the back seat. "We're going to Maryland so you can get married," to which my mother said, "Well, I'm glad someone told me." But she did not protest. Ruthie and Charlie were my parents' witnesses. When recounting this story to me years later, Ruthie said that it took a while to finish the ceremony, because the judge they had found to marry my parents was drunk when they arrived.

After George and Helen returned to Brooklyn, they continued to live apart. Still worried about the stigma of their mixed marriage, they did not tell their families. After they had spent a weekend together in Atlantic City, my grandmother noticed a hotel receipt in my mother's purse.

"You and Georgie are married, aren't you?" she asked my mother. My Polish grandmother always knew my parents were meant to be together. George was devoted to my mother and also to her. He would visit my grandmother whenever my mother and he had had a fight or were supposedly splitting for good. And he always gave my grandmother cash, never wanting her to need for anything. She was well aware that her family in Poland had always been anti-Semitic and that some of her relatives in the United States were the same, but that did not matter to my grandmother. She truly liked George. She knew he was loyal and, most important, she trusted him. "If there were ten naked girls," she used to tell my mother, "Georgie wouldn't look at any of them. It's you he wants."

Eventually, George brought my mother to his sister Harriet's for dinner—but only because Harriet insisted. It was then that my Aunt decided that she would be the one to take my mother to meet their mother, Esther, who lived "down the hill" from Harriet's apartment on Albany Avenue. My tiny, round, Russian grandmother opened the door, wearing an apron, her cheeks flushed from the heat of the oven, her hair in braids pinned on top of her head. She looked at my tall, blonde mother, wearing a large white hat and white summer dress, and said, "You're Georgie's wife." She embraced my mother and, noticing that my mother was not wearing a wedding ring, took off her own and pressed it into my mother's palm.

Had my parents known the introduction would have

been so easy, perhaps they would never have hidden their courtship and could have lived a normal life together a decade earlier. But on that same day, my Jewish grandfather, Joseph, sat brooding in his room, enveloped in darkness— "A self-contemplating shadow/In enormous labours occupied," as poet William Blake writes of his protagonist in the *Book of Urizen*. My grandfather refused to come out to meet this woman his wife had already taken into her heart. It was probably the reaction of his father that George had most feared, although it is amazing to me now that he would have cared so much. His relationship to his father had never been close. But life can be ironic in ways that only reveal over time. Many decades later, after my grandmother died and my grandfather was alone, this same, cold, brooding man who had shunned my mother chose to live with us—as his wife also had done when she was ill—to be certain that my mother, and not his own daughters, would take care of him. And, although George told my mother that his father would never notice, my Catholic mother respected my Orthodox Jewish grandfather's wishes and insisted on keeping a kosher house for him until he died.

My parents had spent their early courtship and married years in New York living the high life. They were always "out on the town." Sometimes they saw two Broadway shows a day—a matinee and then an evening performance. They spent New Year's Eve at the most fashionable restaurants in Manhattan. They were often in nightclubs—as documented by countless sepia-toned photographs— my father, often wearing his army uniform or a dark suit, with his arm around my mother, seated in luxuriously padded leather booths: she, smiling to the camera, a corsage on her lapel and a small hat raked to one side; he, squinting into the bright flashing lights. In these, they both always look gorgeous and exuberant.

When I was a child, my mother still treasured pieces of that glamorous world, the one she lived in before I was born. There were enough items to conjure its romance for me: beaded evening purses with opaline clasps, small velvet hats with polka-dot organza veils, and belts with ivory buckles. I always had the sense that she had been more fabulous, desirable, and elegant than I would ever be, or maybe than the times would ever allow me to become. One day, when she took a navy-blue, fringed, suede belt out of the drawer to show me, it was not so much to revel in its design as it was to reminisce about a time when her waist was so narrow. She was still a tall, beautiful woman then, but no longer as svelte. It was clear that she experienced this change in her body as a great loss. She seemed to long for that life lived in barely lit nightclubs, in the New York that my parents always felt belonged to them. Those years in the city were also a time when men continually pursued her, which was true for her entire life. Once, after George died, my mother, then in her eighties, flew from Florida to visit me in Chicago. She was sitting next to a young businessman who talked to her the entire trip from Fort Lauderdale to O'Hare Airport. At the end of the trip, he asked for her number, but she declined.

George was a professional gambler. As a result, even during the days of the Great Depression, he always had a lot of cash. Before he and my mother had their own apartment together, he shared a room with his brother Hymie in his family's home in Williamsburg. George was careful never to keep his winnings where his mother might find them. He wanted to hide his gambling from my grandmother, channeling money to her through his sisters, but she always knew the money came from George and also how he got it. Still, he was her favorite—funny, loving, and charming. After my parents had been together for some time, George often asked my mother to hold his winnings until the next game—twelve thousand dollars, twenty thousand dollars. He would hand the cash to her in brown paper bags, and she would transfer it to an empty purse, which she would stash in a dresser drawer (a habit she continued her whole life). He would tell her, "Take what you need and hide the rest." She easily could have skimmed off the top—he would never have noticed or cared—but she never did.

When my father said to my mother, "Guess we're not going to that fancy place for dinner tonight," it meant that he had lost at cards or dice, so they would be eating hotdogs at Nathan's in Coney Island instead. When they went to hockey, basketball, and baseball games, they always sat behind home plate. "That's where the betting took place," she told me. Sometimes they went to Sing Sing Correctional Facility in Ossining, New York, where civilians could watch inmates play baseball. My parents often sat high up in the bleachers. As the men walked onto the field, some players recognized my father and would yell out, "Hey George." My mother wondered how he knew so many convicts, but he had been gambling since he was a kid, and New York was a small town then. Loyal to these guys and sorry they got caught, my father always left money with the guards so the men could buy cigarettes in prison.

The start of World War II rocked their world. My mother's five brothers enlisted. My father did not want to go into the military. He tried to get out of it in many ways and hoped his flat feet might do it, but he was able-bodied and, finally, he had no choice. He thought he was emotionally unfit for such service or any other kind of organizational discipline, yet he actually thrived in that environment. He continued to gamble in the barracks and to send earnings back to my mother whenever he could. But gambling would never be the same. "On the boat crossing over the Atlantic to the invasion of North Africa in 1942," he said, "they told us, 'Look to the left, look to the right. Two of you won't be here on the return.'" Then he added, "I didn't like those odds."

George was fortunate to return in one piece. Still, he was gone for four years, a long time, which surely disrupted their life together. My mother once mentioned another man she had liked during the war, someone she had worked with at the Brooklyn Navy Yard while my father was away. There was "distance" between her and my father when he returned from the war, she said. How could there not be? They had both lived through so much and had done so apart. But she never said more.

It must have been difficult for them to settle into life in Crown Heights, especially in that small apartment—domesticated and routinized as the days were then, the nightlife virtually gone and the gambling routines as well. Perhaps that kind of life was no longer exciting to them anyway, or maybe the war had been enough excitement for a lifetime. Still, my mother must have felt lonely for her Polish family and her working life in "the city." Brooklyn was then a small, immigrant, working-class town, and Crown Heights, for the most part, a Jewish urban enclave—his world, to which she had adapted but perhaps hoping for more. They still had many friends from that other life, such as Ruthie and Charlie who lived in Seagate on the beach. (Charlie, once a boxer, then a bookie, had gotten busted while using my parent's first apartment to do business. After that police raid, my parents moved, never explaining to anyone exactly why.) There was also Eddie, a wrestler who still stepped in the ring sometimes. There were the Carnies, who drove my father in his own car from place to place. There was also our Jewish, extended family and all the children and their parents in the building. My parents had settled down, albeit not exactly as other families had—George now working as an auctioneer and a "liquidator and appraiser" late into the night.

In those Crown Heights years while I was growing up, my mother probably felt trapped. She now was at home most days taking care of me, no longer traveling into Manhattan and her life at Evanthes each day. And yet, even after my father died—and to her last days—my mother always said that she had had a "great life" and a "fantastic" husband. "Who could ever want more?"

When my father was drafted into the air force, my mother left Evanthes for a time to support the war effort. Like so many women, she wanted to help in whatever way she could. More than three million women entered the work force between 1940 and 1942, and the country became dependent on female labor. Her friend Rose told her that the shipyards in New Jersey were hiring. My mother soon got a job reading blueprints and waited on Canal Street every day for a ride to Newark. Because gas, like much else, was rationed, people could not fill their own tanks and had to share rides. But my mother eventually became sick with pneumonia because of the cold dampness of the shipyards. When she recovered, she went to work in the Brooklyn Navy Yard, testing computers for submarines. Surprisingly, she had a gift for it, like so many women who discovered unknown aptitudes when they took on these formerly "male" jobs. Her supervisor was surprised at her facility. "When I first saw you," he told my mother, "I thought, what's this glamour girl doing here? But now, honestly, Helen, I've got to say, it takes some men six years to learn what you've mastered in six months." My mother was clever in these ways—able to build almost anything. She understood the physical world and was fearless navigating it.

HASTINGS

In a panoramic photo taken at the navy yard, my mother is with fifty or more of her coworkers—men and women—organized in tiered rows for the camera. She's in the first row, sitting on the floor with one leg bent and the other stretched out, an arm resting on her knee. Now wearing loose, dark overalls and a print bandana tied around her hair, her blonde curls piled on top of her head, she looks relaxed and happy, but soon her youngest brother, Vince, who was a paratrooper, wrote to say that he was about to make a dangerous jump. He asked her to return to Hastings to be with their mother, just in case. My mother knew not to hesitate.

Days after she arrived at the farm, my grandmother awoke one morning and told my mother that she had had a dream: It was raining and there were many dead soldiers lying shoulder to shoulder on wet ground, their faces covered in mud. An officer commanded my grandmother, "Pick out your son." My grandmother knew then that her youngest boy had been killed. Later that morning, my mother heard Josh DiMalach, the neighbor's son, yelling to them as he ran up the hill to their house. Leaning out the window, my mother saw that Josh was waving an envelope. When my grandmother heard him say "a letter for you," she lay down on the bed, turned her face to the wall, and told my mother, "Don't even open it. Vince is dead." My grandmother clutched her heart, and my mother yelled for Josh to get Dr. Early; her mother was having a heart attack.

Vince, whom everyone called Peetsie, was my grandmother's youngest. He was twenty-four years old in 1945. He had already been awarded the Purple Heart for bravery; he died on the southern tip of the Bataan Peninsula on "The Rock" of Corregidor Islands in the Philippines. My grandmother had been three months pregnant with Peetsie when her husband was killed. My Polish grandfather, Joseph, had died alone when the roof collapsed while he was dynamiting a new mine. My grandmother was forty-three or forty-four at the time, with seven other children at home—four boys and three girls. She never remarried, although other Polish miners pursued her, but many of these men, like her husband, drank too much and, when drunk, could be mean, even brutal. She said, "I don't want some man beating up my children." She had had enough of that.

Wielding an ax, my Polish grandfather often threatened my grandmother. He once cornered her in the cellar where they stored canned food and almost killed her, but one of my uncles intervened. In another drunken rage, my grandfather tried to hang himself in the barn, but the rafter he had flung the rope over had not been high enough or strong enough. He was unable to snap his neck. My grandmother then had to send my mother to get her brothers to cut him down. He got the idea after a miner he had been drinking with days before had hung himself from a tree in the woods on his way home from work. That man had used his own necktie to do it, and he had succeeded.

I never knew my Polish grandfather. He was killed before I was born. But in photos taken on the farm he looks as if he were in the backwoods of Poland: he has a large bushy mustache and is wearing high leather boots, a white shirt open at the neck and brown wool pants that flare at the hips. In one photo he wields an enormous scythe.

In the opening sequence of Thomas Hardy's novel, *The Mayor of Casterbridge*, the main character, while drunk, puts his family up as collateral and loses them at a horse auction, apparently not uncommon in the nineteenth century among rural, working-class, drinking men. Likewise, there were rumors that my grandfather had won another family in a card game, early in the twentieth century, some years before my grandmother arrived from Poland to join him in Pennsylvania. That other family lived in a neighboring town where many of our Polish relatives also resided. My grandfather would never visit that town with my grandmother, which convinced her that the rumors were true.

After one of my grandfather's frequent alcoholic binges, he threatened his children with such vehemence that my grandmother yelled to my mother, then eight years old, to run down the road and quickly bring someone back to help. But finding no one at their neighbors' home and terrified that her father might find her and harm her, my mother hid in the neighbor's sitting room. When it got dark and my mother had not yet returned, my extremely worried grandmother sent the family to look for her. Finally, they found her curled up on a green velvet settee in the DiMalach's parlor, asleep.

My mother never talked about the effects of my grandfather's drunken outbursts on her, the trauma they must have caused. But I always suspected that having such a brutal, alcoholic father and fearing for her life and that of her mother and siblings must have caused the split, or dissociation, that I sometimes observed in her during extremely emotional situations. For all her external warmth, generosity, and true love of friends and family, my mother could also seem very detached. This manifested as an impermeable barrier, which I often had encountered when I was a child but also when an adult. There was a coldness and blankness that kept her from bonding with me fully, from engaging me completely, and, most significant to my development, from reflecting me back to myself as being safe in the world. I saw this damage in her most when she suffered loss. At such times, she became overwrought and would often faint from the stress of it. I observed it also in situations where there was conflict, when her full presence was required but could not be summoned, especially when antagonisms arose between my father and me and she was caught between us, uncertain how to respond.

Like Marie, my mother had had a hard start in life, yet she was much more fortunate than Marie. In spite of her abusive father, my mother had a truly loving family of siblings and an extraordinarily devoted and capable mother, whom she adored. There was no question of their closeness, and after my grandfather's mining accident, the siblings bonded together even more tightly in order to survive. The family was extremely poor, but nonetheless my grandmother had taken in two more children who had been abandoned by their parents. The family, now ten, had to be resourceful.

At one time, my Polish grandparents had planned to move to the city, to spare their sons such a hard life in the mines, but when my grandfather was killed, my grandmother stayed in Hastings to raise her family. She used to say, "It is better and healthier to be poor on a farm. At least you can grow your own food, enough to survive." I have thought of this often, especially in the summer months in New York and Chicago, when I have observed families in economically depressed neighborhoods who cannot escape the heat and pollution and have no possibility of raising their own food.

After my grandfather's death, my grandmother received

his forty-dollar-a-month pension, with a reduction as each child grew up and left home. But luckily, she was a good manager. She made sure there were chickens to slaughter or barter; cows and goats to give the family enough milk, butter, and cheese; and an abundance of potatoes to last through the winter and to start the next crop in the spring. My grandmother canned vegetables, fruit, and meat for the winter months. The children picked berries in the summer—some for preserves and some, like elderberries, to sell to winemakers. The family had planted an orchard on their land that my uncles tended, even grafting trees so they had wonderful combinations, cherry-plums and apricot-peaches. My mother's brothers also hunted; there was always plenty of wild game: grouse, pheasant, and venison. When my mother left for New York at sixteen, it was to earn cash to send back home to buy all that they could not grow, hunt, or forage.

My mother feared she would be lonely in the city, but the family soon followed. There was no longer enough work in the mines to employ her brothers. While they were single, they lived with her in a house on Mulberry Street in Lower Manhattan. My grandmother even joined them for a time, but she missed her gardens and soon returned to Hastings. My uncle Jakie and aunt Helen eventually joined her, to manage the farm but also to care for my grandmother until her death.

THE GRANDMOTHERS

I adored both my Polish Catholic and my Russian Jewish grandmothers. They were self-reliant, never complained about their difficult situations, and were incredibly generous and loving to me when I was a child.

My Polish grandmother, Catherine, was powerful and capable, as was my mother, who shared her mother's physical strength, heart-shaped face, and psychic capacity for intuiting what was to come next. She had wonderful vegetable and flower gardens, which she alone tended each day. Like my mother, she too had once been a beautiful woman but, unlike my mother, she had married the wrong man. Perhaps it had been an arranged marriage. She spoke Polish to me when I was a child, and I understood her. But because my parents and I were in New York most of the time, near my Russian Jewish grandmother, Esther—who also lived in Crown Heights and lived longer than Catherine—Esther was more present in my day-to-day life.

Esther and my mother had a deep connection and trust. My grandmother confided to my mother that she had never loved my grandfather. Their marriage had been arranged in Russia before they came to the United States. It was easy to understand why she would not be drawn to my grandfather Joseph. He was taciturn, sullen, and self-absorbed; my grandmother was caring and joyful. It was not a good match. Esther also told my mother that she had once been in love with a boarder that she and her husband had taken into their Williamsburg apartment—a practice common in those days. But with six children and the traditions of an Orthodox Russian Jewish household to uphold, she never could have left.

My Russian grandmother taught my mother to make her favorite recipes: strudel, chicken soup, matzoh balls, pot roast, knishes, Russian-style borscht, and more. She also made wine in the bathtub. Esther saved enough from my grandfather's salary as a tailor and from the money given to her as gifts by her grown children, to invest in gold bracelets, marcasite earrings, and even a small diamond ring, which she bought from a pushcart vendor on Delancey Street in the Lower East Side and left as an inheritance for my mother when she died.

After Esther had her first stroke at eighty, she could no longer speak. Dr. Feinman, our family physician, who lived in a three-story brownstone on President Street, cared for her then. Because my grandparents were aging and my uncle Hymie suffered from gout and arthritis (which ran in my grandmother's family), Dr. Feinman was ever present, taking care of them all. In those days, doctors made house calls. You always knew when doctors were visiting someone in the building because they had special license plates so they could park anywhere—and they often drove Cadillacs.

After my grandmother's stroke, she came to live with us for a time. It was a surprising choice, not lost on her daughters, two of whom had "married well"; lived with their families in much larger, fancier, more comfortable apartments and houses than ours; and had servants who could have cooked kosher meals for my grandmother. But there was no question that when she left the hospital, she would come to stay with her favored—albeit Catholic— daughter-in-law. Although we all wanted my grandmother to be with us (my father adored her), it took some arranging. After my grandmother was established in our only real bedroom, my parents slept on the sofa bed in the living room. But I still wonder, where did I sleep? And now there is no one left to ask.

Dr. Feinman gave me small, flash cards embossed with colored pictures of fruit, vegetables, furniture, and animals. My job was to help my grandmother learn to speak again. Every morning we would prop her up on the bed with many pillows. She was small and round, her gray hair parted into two thin braids that met on top of her head, pinned together with two small rose-shaped barrettes. She wore a pale pink, quilted, satin bed jacket (which became mine after she died and then later fit so well on one of my large, life-size dolls). I would sit on the edge of the bed, and she and I would go through the cards while she tried to say the words that went with the pictures. Because she barely spoke English, my task was even more complex, but also more fun. She found the English words humorous and often mistook a plum with an orange, a cat with a dog. She tried hard to form the sounds, and we laughed when she confused the meanings. But perhaps she knew she was not going to live long enough to learn all these words and only worked so hard to please me.

When we were not engaged with the cards, I would read to her from my favorite books *Sinbad the Sailor*, *Raggedy Ann*, *Babar*, *The Velveteen Rabbit* and help her eat dinner from the tray my mother brought into the room. This was a time of great joy for me, as is often the case when children have an opportunity to feel a sense of purpose and pride because they are able to care for a much-adored adult.

When my grandmother became somewhat stronger, she returned to her own home, which she shared with my grandfather and my uncle Hymie, but she was still quite frail. The night she died, I was already asleep and my mother came into the bedroom and told me that she and my father were going out and that my cousin Bobbie, who was five years older and lived upstairs with her parents— my aunt Harriet and uncle Joe—was coming down to sleep with me. It seemed odd that my parents were leaving at such a late hour, but I quickly fell back asleep. When I woke in the middle of the night, my mother had returned and was closing the blinds in the bedroom, darkening the glare from the streetlights that flooded the room and made patterns on the walls. I heard her sighing, but I only learned the next morning that my grandmother Esther had died.

Many years later, as I was caring for my mother when she was dying in Florida, my mother told me that I reminded her of "Grandma Becker." At first, I took this to mean that, unlike my mother, my Russian grandmother and I were not very tall—but, unlike me, my grandmother was very round. So, I was not sure what she meant, but she soon added, "Your grandmother was a wonderful person." Then I realized that her comment was a true compliment, rare for my mother to offer me and therefore especially memorable. At the time, I took it also to be my mother's acknowledgement of the devotion and care I was offering her.

Because my parents were older when I was born, I lost my grandparents earlier than did most of my friends. My Polish grandmother had been the first to die. Her death probably explains why, at age seven, I wrote a will, assigning all my possessions to my parents and friends. I put that document in a small, flower-decorated, porcelain pitcher on the top shelf of our breakfront in the living room.

When I was young, I was not allowed to go to funerals. My parents undoubtedly thought the experience would be too upsetting for me. But actually, it was my mother who became overwhelmed with grief at such times. I was told that she had fainted at my grandmother Catherine's funeral. The loss of her mother was something she could never talk about without crying, even after she was much older. When my Russian grandfather, Joseph, died, I was in high school, so I was allowed to go to the funeral home the night before the burial. There, I was surprised that my usually dour grandfather was smiling in his casket. I did not understand the logic of this and kept badgering my father to acknowledge how absurd it was that the mortician had chosen to make my grandfather look happy when dead, although he had rarely been so in life. Perhaps my parents had been right to protect me from such rituals.

I adored both grandmothers. And although I had never seen them together, in my mind, they had so much in common. They were from places I had not visited. They spoke languages I did not really speak—Polish, Russian, and Yiddish— but did understand when spoken to. Their strength was clear to me, even then. How had they had the courage to board a ship for a country they had not seen, to live surrounded by a language they never really learned, to begin a future they could barely imagine and then struggle to help their families survive when there were so few material resources? Both had married men who had brought them unhappiness, but they knew how to love their children and they both loved me unequivocally, so when I lost them, the sadness was immense.

THE JEWISH-CATHOLIC DILEMMA

Although I moved fluidly between the Jewish and Catholic families, I was deeply aware of the complexity of my own identity, but my parents only really addressed the subject directly with me once. I must have been about thirteen years old when George asked me to go outside with him. It was summer, and he was wearing chino pants and a gray-and-white-striped, short-sleeved shirt. We sat in front of Peck Memorial Hospital across the street from our building and perched on a hill. A large swinging gate allowed ambulances to drive up the path to the hospital at any hour but also gave access to those in the neighborhood who wanted to enter. He and I had brought two multicolored, woven-plastic, aluminum beach chairs from the apartment (ubiquitous among our neighbors at that time). We placed the chairs against the railing, away from the street and therefore away from the noise on Albany Avenue. In this position, we were directly across from our apartment and would have been clearly visible to my mother. I did not yet know what the topic was going to be but I did understand that this would be an important conversation.

I realize now that my father was the parent designated to raise the topic of religion with me. He was an odd choice to initiate this discussion because he always seemed apathetic and even irreverent about Judaism. My parent's marriage was, of course, a serious defiance of the rules set by his very orthodox father. But, in practice, religion did not play a role in my father's daily life, nor in that of my Catholic mother. And although there was deep anxiety around their mixed marriage (or they would not have hidden it from their families for so long), this subject also, was never discussed. They obviously feared the anti-Semitism of the Polish family and the tribalism of the Jewish one and they did not want to be ostracized by either. And although I did have some intuitive understanding of this complexity, I did not yet understand the history of Poland's complicity with the Nazis during the war, or even know that Auschwitz—a name too familiar to us all at the time—was located in Poland. But I did understand something of the tensions that my identity embodied.

I was a *mishling,* a mix or half-breed—in those days, the near equivalent to biracial. One of my Polish Catholic cousins seemed to enjoy telling me that my mother and I surely would "burn in Hell." But I never really believed it or even understood what that would mean, at least not consciously. I did not tell my parents the things he said to me. I already understood that he was provincial, knew no other Jewish people, and lived only surrounded by Catholics.

My father never went to synagogue, which I did, and he had not learned to read Hebrew very well, which I had. My Jewish grandfather told me that my father had been thrown out of every Hebrew school in Brooklyn (probably an exaggeration) but he surely had been barred from at least a few close by in Williamsburg, likely because he was so uninterested in preparing for his Bar Mitzvah. My grandfather finally had to find a rabbi in New Jersey who had not yet heard about my father. George, I was told, then learned just enough to get through the ceremony.

Yet, after my grandmother and my uncle Hymie died, my father read the Kaddish—the mourner's prayer for the dead—for an entire year on their behalf. He also wore a rent piece of black grosgrain ribbon on his shirt lapel to designate that he was in mourning. Our apartment was so small that, as my father stood in the foyer saying the prayer softly to himself each morning, I could hear every word from my bed in the living room. Some of his early training had stuck. He probably was reading the prayer phonetically, but it sounded good to me.

So, on that day in front of Peck Memorial Hospital, I knew that religion was not a topic my father would ever willingly have engaged in with me. My mother must have insisted that now was the time for us to have this conversation. I also imagine that she was watching us from our small kitchen window across the street, wondering how it was going.

The conversation was about me and my future. There would come a day, my father said, when I would have to choose between Judaism and Catholicism—probably when I got married, he conjectured, and certainly when I had children and needed to decide how they would be raised. He laid out the situation but did not offer any advice about how to think about it. To him it was just a dilemma for me to consider and for which someday, I would have to find a solution, although my parents had not. They had never chosen one religion over another for me. Instead, they had left me alone to immerse myself in both religions as much as I could while we celebrated all holidays equally. We had a Christmas tree each year—the only one at 424 Albany Avenue at that time. Some children in our building came down to decorate the tree with us, and we saved all the decorations in a big box from one year to the next—the shiny ornaments and the cottony floor covering that surrounded the tree with a blanket of fake glittery snow. There also was Hanukkah and Passover with my Jewish grandfather, and Sabbath candles for me to light each week; I never wanted to miss an opportunity to say the prayers in Hebrew.

Because I was born on Easter Sunday, and my birthday falls on this holiday every eleven years, Easter too was always an important celebration. I received baskets filled with Barton's solid-chocolate bunnies, frozen in profile and carved like statues, that took weeks to consume (I was never sure where to begin . . . the ears or the tail?).

My mother carried rosary beads and the cards of saints in her purse, even to the very end of her life. I doubt that she ever went to church however, except for the few times when we reluctantly joined the Polish relatives in Pennsylvania for Sunday Mass or happened to pass an open church and could light a candle for a family member or friend who was ill, dying, or had just passed away. Because my mother never converted to Judaism, I am technically not Jewish (although had I been born in Nazi Germany, I certainly would have been considered so). But none of this ever seemed to matter to me or to us.

I immersed myself in Jewish traditions and learned the (perhaps apocryphal) admonition: if you were chosen to carry the Torah through the synagogue on Simchat Torah (in those days, at our shul women never were) and you dropped it, you would have to carry it on your back for the rest of your life. Even then I wondered, who invented such rules? Still, on Yom Kippur my friends and I fasted and went to services with Mrs. Goldstein. We did not even drink water and pretended, for that one day a year, that we were orthodox. Later we walked around the neighborhood dressed in too-tight, strapless, patent leather shoes. I did all this while reading books about the lives of saints and from time to time, placing rosary beads in my shoes to torment myself as the saints had done, while trying to understand the enigma of the Holy Ghost. Living this dual, spiritual life within the complexity of two distinct religions had never seemed a problem—yet, there we were, my father and I, sitting on those brightly colored beach chairs, imagining a moment in time when I would have to make a real decision about religion, a conundrum for which, even then, I knew there would never be a solution.

I do not remember how I felt during or after this conversation or precisely what was said, although the ambiguity of the discussion and the sense of impending action obviously resonated with me at the time and haunts me still. The implication of making a choice between two religions had several elements. It meant choosing father over mother; one set of beloved aunts, uncles, and cousins over the other; urban over rural. Although I did finally identify more with Brooklyn and Judaism, probably because I lived most of my childhood in Crown Heights and spent more time with my Jewish relatives than with my Catholic ones, I did love both families and locations.

My perception of my class standing was also distorted by the comparisons between my Jewish and Catholic relatives. As a child, it seemed to me that my parents and I had much greater material resources than my rural Catholic cousins, but in fact our resources were only different. My family in Pennsylvania had a farm, animals, and freedom of movement in nature—all of which I reveled in with great exuberance when with them. But the Jewish world of Brooklyn actually was more modern and prosperous than the farms and mining towns of western Pennsylvania. When my Catholic cousins came to New York, they were obsessed with our flush toilets and running water. None of this made us rich by any objective standards, but if you had a well, a pump, an outhouse, and a coal stove, as they did—as we all did when there for the summers—it appeared that those of us in New York had so much more. As a result, whenever these cousins visited, my mother felt obliged to give them whatever she could. At times these were things that belonged to me— toys, dolls, clothes, books—that she thought they could use and that I no longer needed. It was painful to have these things taken from me and to appear as a selfish child if I objected or, at times, cried at their loss. But because my mother had grown up so poor, she believed I was spoiled by an excess of belongings and thought it was best to help me rid myself of some of them.

At 424 Albany Avenue, no one really had more than anyone else, so we did not compare wealth or envy each other or long for things out of reach. And in truth, we all did have enough. But because my father was an auctioneer, we just seemed to float above the normal patterns of wanting and buying, so I always felt we had more than others. Later when I was in graduate school in Southern California and a member of a Women's Liberation group, we were asked to define our "class origins." It was then that I recognized, for the first time, that my comprehension of my class situation had been skewed by the sociological differences between my families and also by my access to more "stuff" than others living in our Crown Heights building. Listening to this group of women, I finally understood that, having grown up in a three-room apartment, with a gambler-auctioneer father who never finished high school and a hairdresser mother from the farm whose education only went as far as fifth grade, did not make me upper middle class as I had always thought, but rather, probably more economically working class and culturally marginal than anything else.

Ultimately, the preference of religion was a matter of choosing those spiritual narratives that resonated most deeply with my psyche. Orthodox Judaism captured my child's heart because it was bacchanalian and joyful, and the services held in Hebrew were dramatic and mysterious to me. But later, I became entranced by Renaissance painting and its religious iconography and infinite representations of the Virgin and Child as well as the saints. Judaism, which prohibits representational imagery, could never compete in these visually, extravagant ways.

Something else also separated me from Catholicism and helps explain my reluctance to embrace it fully. In the 1950s, another deadly flood (the first had been in 1889) devastated Johnstown, Pennsylvania, a city close to Hastings. I learned about the scale of the damage during one of the few times I did attend church with my Polish cousins. The priest's sermon focused on this event and then asked each family present to donate a sizable portion of their earnings to help the victims. My Catholic relatives left the church quite unsettled. His request was the main subject of the car ride home: how could they give so much to others when they had so little themselves? Perhaps unjustifiably, I resented the priest for putting them in what seemed to me a humiliating position.

Ironically, I never have had to make a choice between Judaism and Catholicism. If asked now, I probably would call myself a Buddhist, but even that would not be absolute. I do identify as Jewish if I identify with religion at all, but, in fact, I live in a multifarious universe of spiritual ideas and have found important lessons and true resonance in many traditions. Perhaps when you are raised in two religions, you can never really be a purist about faith or almost anything else. I am grateful there was so much religion in my childhood—enough to fill a true hunger for a complex spiritual life.

Having lived my early years in the shadow of such an unresolvable dilemma, to this day I can easily become immobilized when pressured to make complex decisions too quickly. Perversely, it is not always the life-altering decisions that I find daunting, it is often rather the more inconsequential ones. Still, I attribute these moments of numbing ambivalence and, at times, wrenching anxiety, to this originary conversation with my father, after which I began to fear that on some unspecified day—ready or not—I would be forced to make an enormous, irrevocable choice that might bring great sorrow to me and to others while catalyzing unanticipated consequences.

MY MOTHER AND ANDY WARHOL

When I was older, my mother returned to work at Evanthes. But everything there had changed—the clientele and the neighborhood. Times Square was now rundown and sketchy; nonetheless my mother was excited to be out in the world again. Celebrities surprisingly still came for "treatments" or color—a new bunch. U.S. Representative Bella Abzug's husband was a client (which is how my mother got to know Bella and was often invited to political receptions in her honor). The cast of The Carol Burnett Show were clients, and a new group of "showgirls and boys" came up, needing to quickly become blonds, redheads, or brunettes, depending on the casting call of the day.

For some, it was not really the "treatments" that brought them back, but rather the chance to relax and receive the solicited and unsolicited personal advice and counseling my mother and Marie gave so generously. But the artist Andy Warhol, "Andy" as my mother always referred to him, definitely came for the wigs. I used to tell people that my mother made wigs for Andy Warhol, but that was not entirely correct. Mercedes, her coworker, actually made the wigs while my mother and Marie still gave clients, including Warhol, "scalp treatments" with the ultraviolet wand.

The first time my mother met Warhol he was sitting on one of the shop's leather-covered barber's chairs and had his back to her. "That's Andy," her boss told her. "He's here for a treatment." As my mother approached Warhol with the wand, he turned around and said, "Wait a minute, let me take off my wig." That's when she saw that he was almost bald. "Andy only had a fringe around his head," my mother told me. "For a young guy he was quite bald. It took one girl working full-time to keep up with the toupees. He needed two a month, she said, "all natural— 'virgin' hair, never dyed, a mix of white, platinum, and gray." She often wondered what he did with all those wigs until she read in a society column that he had thrown a party at which guests were each given tufts of hair to glue to their bodies. Then she thought she understood. This part of the story always made her chuckle to herself, as if telling a joke whose punch line only she could understand.

My mother and Warhol were both from immigrant families in Pennsylvania that had not yet assimilated. They were first generation, although she was decades older. He was from Pittsburgh, she from Hastings, near Altoona. His mother was Slavic (Carpatho-Rusyn), from what is now Eastern Slovakia; hers was Polish. They were not "modern," as my mother would explain—both their mothers wore babushkas. He spoke a Slavic language or dialect to his mother; she spoke Polish to hers. My mother was Roman Catholic. He was raised as Byzantine Catholic. When Warhol's mother came to Evanthes with him, my mother spoke Polish to her, and, my mother said, she "seemed to understand." I doubt my mother ever knew or suspected how really close Warhol was to his mother or that his mother was also a very talented artist, who, some have said, was brilliant and often collaborated with her son.

My mother was not sophisticated about intellectual ideas and made no pretensions of understanding the art world, which was quite unknown to her, but "Andy," the person, as she experienced him, seemed very familiar to her, although she did recognize his uniqueness. But this sense of familiarity gave my mother license (although she never really needed it) to offer him her opinions about life, as if he were her nephew or her son. She also definitely had affection for him and felt protective of him. But she did not and could not have understood his creative complexity or his place in a downtown art scene that she had never experienced and about which she had little curiosity.

Of course, she knew that he was famous and she was proud of him for that. He had worked hard to succeed. She understood it was not easy to come to New York from an immigrant family and do so well. He had made money; he was well known and admired. Many were trying to achieve what he already had. Although much was strange to her, she did understand that "Andy" had figured it out.

But her way of talking about him was to make fun of his eccentricity. She told me that, "Sometimes he would come in wearing one brown shoe, one black shoe. I would say, 'Andy, you have two different shoes on.' 'Do I?' he would ask. He was like that." He was "almost in a dream, but he was never demanding." He preferred to arrive at Evanthes early, before they opened, or late, after they closed. He never wanted to be seen. The staff liked his shyness. They experienced enough flashy types.

When Warhol first started coming up to Evanthes, he was working for Helena Rubenstein. "A good publicity agent had put him at all the right parties," my mother said, "got his name circulated." But in her opinion, he always was surrounded by "strange people." She had seen his brother, John Warhola, painting with chicken claws on TV. "Another odd one," she said. Using one of her favorite expressions, she described Warhol as "homely as sin." Marie would add, "Can you imagine waking up to that?"

CAROL BECKER

But no matter what disparaging statements had preceded, they always made sure to follow with a comment about how "very good-natured he was," "a real gentleman," "extremely kind to his nephews"—these were the things that mattered to them, those they understood. They knew he lived in a different world, a world they did not engage. But because he had always been kind to them, they were loyal to him. As my mother said, "Andy and I didn't talk much. There was not enough in common—and, of course, he was so shy."

When my mother read in the paper that Warhol had bought cases of Campbell's tomato soup, she asked him, "Andy, what are you going to do with all that soup?" "My friends and I will eat it, Helen, don't worry," he said. He probably understood how odd this seemed to her, knew how poor they all had been and what having food had meant for her and his mother's generation and for their mothers' generation too. But he never made Marie or my mother feel stupid or judged. My mother and Marie understood that those in the know thought he had something special, they just didn't understand what that was or why it was so valuable—in the same way that many people are often confused by the contemporary art scene. Nonetheless, Paul Evanthes always hoped Warhol would give him a painting, but he never did.

My mother was a New Yorker, which meant that she had seen a great deal and was not easily undone, but she was not at all savvy about art and definitely not about the avant-garde. One day she convinced Marie that they should go to a Warhol film that was playing on 42nd Street. My mother often saw "foreign films," as she called them, at the Thalia or at other New York art-house theaters. Although she could be cruel and mock what she did not understand, she was more open, cosmopolitan, and generous to what was unfamiliar or unconventional to her than one might have guessed from such behavior—but this Warhol film daunted her. As she described it, "The movie started, and there was a woman sitting in a rocking chair—rocking, rocking, and a Victrola going around and around, screeching—no music. There was also a bird or something, squawking." After half an hour, when, in her observation, nothing was happening, she said to Marie, "I'm going to get our money back."

"You wouldn't dare," Marie said.

But she did dare and she did succeed, as had others who witnessed Warhol films for the first time and had asked for the same. "We were big girls in those days," my mother said, "and in our winter coats, we looked even bigger. "The theater manager probably thought we were women cops." The next day Paul asked, "Helen, how was the movie?"

"Paul," she said, likely shaking her head in incredulity, "If you saw it, you'd say this guy is crazy. How can he put out such garbage? It wasn't obscene or anything—just stupid. You know how a record can keep turning and turning but nothing comes out? It was like that."

She once asked me, "Do you know about that warehouse Andy had?"

"You mean the Factory?" I asked.

"I wonder if they ever cleaned up all the crap?" she said. "That junk's probably worth a fortune now."

The Andy Warhol who was revered for his genius was unknown to my mother, and even if she had had the chance to learn more about why he was considered so seminal to contemporary art, she would not have understood what all the fuss was about. She did not move in the world of the abstract or the conceptual. She would probably be shocked to know the enormous influence that Warhol has had on generations of artists and what the work is worth now. This world was not her world, although it became mine.

"He wasn't ever a well man," my mother said about Warhol, "sickly, really, from childhood—scarlet fever, I think—and being shot, well, that certainly didn't help any." In 1968 after Valerie Solanas shot Warhol and he was in the hospital, Paul Evanthes went there every two weeks to change his wigs because, as my mother explained, "Andy always liked them fluffy."

I told her that in *I Shot Andy Warhol,* the movie about Solanas, the actor who plays Warhol wears a wig that does not fit well, and his dark hair is visible underneath, especially after the actor is "shot" and has fallen to the floor. This information distressed her. "That's inauthentic," she said, "Andy's wigs came down all the way, definitely. We would never have made them like that. The wigs were put on with double-sided tape—one side to the wig, the other to the scalp, then glued, so they wouldn't blow off, and they couldn't ever move. He only had a fringe around the bottom, and it was stringy," she added. "He didn't really have any of his own hair to speak of." But in video clips of Warhol from this time, it is clear that at least some of his wigs did not come "down all the way," and there was a dark fringe on the bottom—perhaps a look he cultivated later. Those wigs also probably were not made at Evanthes.

Years later, after George died and my mother was still living in Tamarac, Florida, she often went back to New York to see her friends. The noise and pollution of the city were too stressful for her then, but the hot Florida summers were also intolerable, so she came north. And for at least one night during that time, she always stayed with Marie, who lived in a very small apartment in the then subsidized Stuyvesant Town. If she did not make time to spend with Marie, Marie would feel hurt and then angry. "You only go with the rich," Marie once told my mother, referring to my parent's good friend Sarah, who had owned buildings in Flatbush in Brooklyn and who lived in a large apartment on 10th Street in the East Village, between University and Third Avenue, where my mother sometimes stayed.

Marie and my mother had always gambled together, in any form they could—the way those who never had enough or were unable to earn enough often did, keeping alive the dream of someday becoming instantly rich. At one time, they bet on the horses, especially during all those years at Evanthes, when clients who were trainers regularly gave them inside tips. My mother once tried to set me up with one of those trainers she liked a lot. Whatever horse he told her to bet on, she would. If she gave him twenty dollars to put on a horse, he often brought her back two hundred, saying that she had won. I often wondered if she really had or if he just hated to see her and Marie lose. Surely those races were fixed, and he was on "the inside," so perhaps the tips he gave them were always "for sure" bets.

In their later years, there were no more trips to Las Vegas or to Atlantic City with my mother's nieces to play the slot machines. Because she and Marie moved more slowly at this stage, the gambling had to be easy to get to or it did not happen at all. In Stuyvesant Town, therefore, it was Bingo in the recreation room. Marie played every day and often won. She could track fifteen cards at a time, easily. My mother, however, was hooked on the lottery and had no interest in Bingo—for her, the stakes were simply too low.

George

George had flair. Tall, confident, handsome, with black hair and blue eyes, he lived in a world of carnies, boxers, hustlers, and hard-working, independent, small-business street guys of New York, like himself. There was always at least one of these types driving him around the boroughs, to his stores, warehouses, or other sites of business. They were not chauffeurs, exactly—he neither had the money nor the car for that—just men working for him, who, as he would say, were "not too smart" but were willing to be paid to do what my father hated most: drive and park the car. My mother read voraciously—any novel she could acquire. She subscribed to "Reader's Digest Condensed Books," a series of shortened versions of all the classics. But my father, who loved a good story and was a terrific storyteller, almost never read books. In our apartment, there was only one that belonged to him: the famous true-crime exposé *Murder, Inc.: The Story of the Syndicate*, published in 1951, about a string of organized-crime murders that began in Brooklyn. I am certain he was drawn to it because he was acquainted with quite a few of the main characters.

George, always a gambler, had been kicked out of high school for "shooting craps"— almost everything, for him, had something to do with calculating "the odds." He was smart, especially with numbers, fast-talking, naturally funny, and, within the petty dishonesties of the marginal worlds he inhabited, trustworthy. He was known to some as "Honest George." And so, he was—a charismatic guy who sparkled with life, except when worrying too much about business, and a person for whom the laws of the street were absolute. You were either with him, on his side completely, or you were not. And when you were not, the doors shut behind you, forever.

George had no patience with conventional institutions and felt no need to prove himself to them. And yet, remarkably, he had done well in the army. After he was made a sergeant in the air force, his superiors wanted to send him for officer training, but that was not for him. Always his own person, he was someone others naturally followed. His men loved him, and they stayed in touch for more than fifty years, always exchanging Christmas and New Year's cards. He was especially close to his friend Johnny. In the framed sepia photograph I have lived with my whole life, George and Johnny are both dressed in their uniforms, balancing their pointed, boat-shaped flight caps on their heads, standing in front of a palm tree in North Africa: my father: gangly, relaxed, a cigarette in his right hand, as always, with his left arm draped comfortably around Johnny's neck; Johnny: a handsome Italian, some inches shorter than my father, with a fashionably small mustache. Forty years after that photo was taken, when my parents were living in Florida, they received a Christmas card from Johnny's wife. My mother opened the card first. It was glittery, with a reindeer flying over small red brick houses flecked with snow. His wife had written inside that Johnny had died that past spring. My mother hid the card from my father and never told him what she had learned. She knew it would upset him too much.

When George returned from the war, he looked for some respectable work to do. He teamed up with his brother, my uncle Hymie, and they went into the auction business together, buying up stores that were failing or those whose owners wanted to close shop. They would "lot up" all the merchandise, organize the stock into categories, and sell some of the goods right out from these stores; they could then legally post "going out of business" signs in the windows and radically discount the prices for one month. They also rented other outlet spaces and sold merchandise from these businesses at a reduced rate until all was gone. If there was stock left over, or if they happened to buy a big lot of dry goods, they would hold auctions in rented warehouse spaces to sell it to storeowners.

Early on, George was the auctioneer—the man "up on the block." He was good at that fast-talking auctioneer patter. I never did know how he had learned it. Before the auction, he would send out postcards to announce the time and place to his lists of owners of hardware or dry goods stores in the boroughs. When I was about eight years old and still had a very clumsy child's hand, he often hired me to address these postcards. He did not seem to care or even notice how the cards looked. If anyone had ever noted their awkwardness, perhaps mentioning they looked "as if a child had addressed them," no one ever told me. I was proud to get paid for each card.

These auctions often happened in big, cold, damp warehouse spaces that smelled of mildew. I was sometimes invited to be a "shill" on the floor. A business friend of my father's or my uncle Hymie himself always stood next to me and told me when to raise my hand. Everyone knew

I was George's daughter and surely got a kick out of my presence there, as did I.

Although I understood little about the business then, when friends from the building came over to play, the game of choice—my choice, of course—was "auctioneer." I had clipboards with yellow pads attached (which George had brought home for me). Everyone would get a set to work with and a sharpened pencil. I would pull all my toys out of my toy chest in the foyer and from under the bed, and we would "lot up" the merchandise into categories, writing down the quantity of each: three large dolls, eight small ones, two Babar books, and so forth. There was no real tension in this game, no winning, no losing, no challenge. I can see that now, but playing at my father's work kept him close to me.

We were living on Albany Avenue then, and during those years my father and I played five-card open-hand poker for fun but also to bet on things I wanted. If I said I desperately needed a new bike or new skates (roller or ice), he would bring out the deck. We would sit in the living room at the mahogany table—the one with the raised, gold fleur-de-lis border—that always smelled of lemon-scented furniture polish. And, to prove we were serious, we would put on our stiff, black-leather visors, as if to shield ourselves from an imaginary single light bulb hanging from a ceiling, like the one I had seen in the 1955 film, *The Man with the Golden Arm*. Thus attired, we would begin the game.

George, experienced as he was, always cut the deck, either with "the fan," shuffling the cards in and out like an accordion; with "the spring," pressing a thumb down on each half of the deck and then releasing and merging the stacks one into the other, at least three times; or with "the bridge," raising the cards up into an arch, positioning them for a controlled fall, and dividing them into piles. Finally, he would cut the cards once more, flicking them up from the bottom to blend them together.

Having played poker for his livelihood, George must have been in many games that looked like those we now see only in movies. But playing cards with me was theatrical and joyful for him. He loved to set the stage and to act the part, but we were always very serious. He wanted me to learn "to stare him down," to not reveal my hand or the moves I was about to make. He also wanted me to "play to win." In his way he taught me to take risks, not to be intimidated, to play the game well, literally and figuratively, to control the outcome as best I could, and to have fun along the way. I have always thought that part of the reason I could engage boards of governors and trustees —comprised almost entirely of male corporate CEOs and university presidents— in my roles as dean and vice president, without ever being intimidated, was because of this early training from my father. As educated and successful as these men were, to me none were ever as tough, as confident, as clever, or as much fun as my father. If I could be his equal, I surely could be theirs. Years later, when I was studying Shotokan Karate and other forms of martial arts, I learned not to blink when I was about to throw a punch. If you blink, as we all instinctively want to do, you forfeit the advantage of surprise. I had already learned early, and literally, to maintain a "poker face" and "keep my cards close to my chest"–useful training for me, who, in the future, would have to negotiate with many different kinds of people.

If I won the card game, I got whatever I was asking for; if I lost, I usually got it anyway, although I might have to wait a bit until my father or uncle bought out a store that had the desired object in it. In those days, we did not shop for most things, other than food and clothing. We just waited until what we wanted or needed appeared in inventory. My father and my uncle once bought out a store because there was a red girl's Schwinn bicycle in the window. When they brought the bike home, they wanted to surprise me and so they left it standing in the living room for me to happen upon. But because I knew how things worked, I had already been imagining that a new bike would appear one day if I were patient.

On my birthday every year during high school, when we were living in Flatbush, George would bring out an enormous jar filled with quarters he had been hiding under the floorboards of his closet all year. He would put the jar on the small pink Formica table in the kitchen. Next to it he would place a Ben Franklin one-hundred-dollar bill. I had the choice to either choose the bill or the quarters. I always chose the quarters. Of course, I also always hoped I had gambled correctly. I was too much my father's daughter not to want to win. George would often wait to bring out the jar until a cousin, aunt, or neighbor was visiting, someone who could help me and my mother stack the quarters on the table into little dollar piles of four and who would also enjoy the game of it. Sometimes George would call across our backyard and ask one of our neighbors, the Napolis, to drop by, just for this purpose. The more people involved in the process, the more fun it was. When the jar was empty, and piles of quarters covered the table, we would count the stacks. If the quarters fell short of one hundred dollars, I could pretty much be certain George would make up the difference. He would then take the quarters to the bank, exchange them for bills for me and start collecting quarters again, to be ready for my birthday the following April.

George worked late into the evenings, buying up merchandise of stores in what seemed to be remote locations, from a Crown Heights, Brooklyn, perspective— places I had never heard of, like Hackensack and Paramus, New Jersey; Yonkers and Poughkeepsie, New York; and neighborhoods in the Bronx and Staten Island. If he found something that he thought I might like, we would go together to the store or warehouse on a weekday night or weekend day to look at it together, stopping at his new "favorite" diner or Chinese restaurant on the way home. The neighborhoods were usually run down and often quite unsafe—men hanging out on dimly lit corners surrounded by broken glass from smashed streetlights. After opening several padlocks and closing metal accordion gates, we finally were safe inside. These storage areas were always piled dangerously high with cardboard boxes, dust was everywhere: on every object, in the air, and on the countertops. I tried not to touch too many things or rub against the shelving. My father would hand me a bag or a box and tell me to "take whatever" I wanted. When I was in sixth grade, he once bought out a toy store that had been through a fire. Everything there was covered with dirt and smelled of smoke. I filled a basket with dolls' clothes (for the then-popular Ginny dolls, the innocent, flat-chested, prepubescent precursors to Barbie). Back home, I washed, hung to dry, and ironed those miniature outfits, selling them at a school-wide UNESCO children's drive the following week.

My father floated through merchandise of all kinds—some worth little and some worth quite a bit. He did not personally care about the tools or clothes or antiques he found. He was not a collector nor an aficionado of vintage objects, antiques, or discontinued items. These things might be treasures for some, but not for him. In his eyes, it was all "junk." His business was commerce, and his job was to acquire what others might want and to make a profit by moving it on and out. There was no nostalgia or romance to any of this. From time to time, however, something would catch his eye and he would bring it home, especially when we lived in East Flatbush and had more space to display or store things. When he bought out the entire stock of ceramic dinnerware from the famous restaurant Ruby Foo's, we had wonderful blue-and-white serving platters, round and oval, with metal lids to keep the food warm. We also had elegant coconut-shaped cups from which customers once drank Mai Tais. When he eventually bought out the fixtures of Lundy's seafood restaurant in Sheepshead Bay, we had plates shaped like red lobsters and some shaped like shrimp. We also had long, yellow, textured dishes that simulated corncobs and, to pair with them, little plastic pincers, shaped like miniature cobs, that helped us hold the hot corn.

In these ways, I grew up among objects, most of them practical and some what we might now consider kitsch. Mostly they had no real artistic value, but they were curiosities, cultural artifacts that others I knew simply did not have. Perhaps because there was so much of it, it all had little value for George. There would always be more— another warehouse full of merchandise, an endless supply. But I reveled in these objects and have some of them still.

By immersing myself in the worlds of art and culture as I have done in my adult life in various positions as professor of the arts and deans of art schools, I have learned a great deal about the making of objects which are fascinating because they are fabricated by artists and artisans whose visual expertise they embody. I grew to appreciate and to be curious about such inventions, enough to study them and experience them in museums, galleries, and studios around the world. I became especially interested in objects that reflect a historical moment. Perhaps I have always been intrigued by the enormous range of things that we as humans design for practical reasons but also for play, to embellish our environments, to reflect a particular moment and to amuse and at times aggrandize ourselves. But none of that sensibility came directly from my family. Such ideas were not what my parents thought about or discussed, and they only became part of my life later.

On weekends, when he could spare the time, George and I would visit his family. My grandmother and grandfather lived close to us in Crown Heights. Their small, immaculately clean apartment, was furnished with overstuffed, dark-green velour couches and mahogany tables that looked very "European" to my child's eye. My Russian grandfather was a tailor in the garment district on Manhattan's Lower East Side. He worked in a factory every day into his eighties, until he was assaulted by a mugger one snowy morning, knocked down on the ice, unable to get back up. After that, the family insisted that he stop working.

My father's three sisters lived in different parts of Brooklyn. Harriet, who had helped my parents find our apartment, was my favorite and probably the closest to George. She also was the youngest. When she was an infant, my father had once traded her for a puppy while he was supposed to be watching her in her carriage. Because

Harriet's skin color was dark, the kids taunted him about her, using a racist Yiddish word for "black person." So, when offered the puppy, he exchanged my aunt outright. My grandmother, who told me the story, would recall how terrified she had been when she went outside to check on them and could not find her baby, who, it turned out, had been taken to a strange home by a small boy, whose mother was equally distraught by the situation until it was finally sorted out.

My father's sister Sadie was the oldest. She and her husband, Nathan, lived in a doorman building on Eastern Parkway across from the Brooklyn Museum. They owned what my parents always referred to as "the best children's clothing store in Brooklyn." It was called Boxers, after my uncle, Nathan Boxer, and was located on Pitkin Avenue, not far from Crown Heights. That store, with its racks of gorgeous children's clothing, was where I developed my taste for well-designed outfits that we probably could never have afforded had we not gotten the family discount. Because of Boxers, I always had a fabulous new wool coat—with a velvet or chinchilla collar—for the Jewish holidays, a special dress for my birthdays, and, each year, a new straw hat embellished with linen flowers to wear as we watched those in the annual New York Easter Parade march down Fifth Avenue.

Julia, my father's third sister, lived in a large brick house on Flatbush Avenue. She had married well. Her husband, Ben, went into the nylon stocking business early, when synthetic stockings first hit the market in the late 1930s. At that time, silk from Japan was hard to find and prohibitively expensive when you could; nylon was the future.

My aunt Julia and uncle Ben also owned a bungalow in the Rockaways, on a sandy street near the beach, surrounded by juniper trees where they grew Concord grapes and strawberries. From time to time, we would visit them there. My aunt had an array of knickknacks and antiques carefully arranged on a shelf above the fireplace. On one of our visits, my father, who was pigeon-toed and sometimes a bit off-balance, bent down to retrieve something he had dropped near the fireplace. When he stood up, oblivious to what was above him, he inadvertently raised the shelf with his back, and all the objects crashed to the floor, rolling under the couch and tables—a cacophony of breaking porcelain and reverberating metal. Unfazed by the chaos, he surveyed the situation, and, laughing at himself and the mess he had caused, said to my aunt, "Don't worry about this junk. I'll get you more. I've got some real antiques in my store right now, and you can have your pick."

The sisters knew him well. So, after they absorbed the shocks of such innocent fiascos, they would simply shrug, sigh, roll their eyes, and exclaim, "Georgie." But they never did get angry at him. They knew the breadth of his generosity. He often brought them to his stores when he thought there might be something they or their children, might like or could use. He then would say to them, as he always did to me, "Take whatever you want."

Of the three brothers—George, Max, and Hymie— the sisters loved George best. Their eldest brother, Max, was absent and detached. He married and divorced the same woman twice, Claire, whom no one had really liked the first time. Max never seemed to care much for the family, did not visit his father often (although my grandfather always talked about him, his first born). Hymie was the sweetest of them all but he was sick a good deal of the time with gout and arthritis, and they worried about him. George, the youngest, playful and handsome, was irresistible. And because they knew that he liked sweets, they always stocked their houses for his visits.

So, after the wreckage he caused in the Rockaways, his pockets stuffed with silver-wrapped chocolate kisses that had filled the no-longer-intact glass bowl on the end table, we were off to the city. En route, we stopped for ice cream sodas: chocolate soda with strawberry ice cream for him; chocolate soda with coffee ice cream for me. He had a sweet tooth, and so do I.

Although my father appeared easygoing, even carefree, with his restless, playful spirit, always wanting to be in two places at the same time, ready for adventures, I knew he was a worrier. His worries were mostly about money because he never made all he had hoped he would. "I wanted you to be an heiress," he once said to me wistfully, pronouncing the h as in hair. "I wanted to leave you a lot of money." Although an inheritance surely never concerned me, it did him. Were he young now, he might do well in some loft space in Bushwick, Brooklyn, with a few employees, answering to no one, cooking up something new. He had the concept of the urban "dollar store" in the 1950s, and then the suburban outlet or home and garden store in the early '60s. But he never really had the financial backing to make them work, although he tried. When these innovations did manifest in the world, they were big for some, even for his nephew, Bob Rickel in New Jersey, but not for George and not then. He truly had an independent, entrepreneurial, start-up mentality, but all too early. When these possibilities did not succeed, his sense of personal failure wore him down and seeped into my consciousness as well. It was never the money itself that haunted me, but the weight of its absence on him.

Money was also how my father understood the world. As a child and as an adult, if I tried to explain something complex to him, he would say, "Tell it to me in dollars and cents," which meant, say it straight, plain, clear, no frills, in terms I can understand. When I was in college, he would say, "Stop using those dollar words," which is how he referenced my growing vocabulary and use of three-syllable words. To his way of thinking, money was the measure of all things, and he simply never had made enough. "It's harder and harder for a small businessman to survive in this country," he would say. "The taxes kill you." As a child, I never really understood how he experienced that reality each day or what it meant for the future of our country. But the fact that he worried, worried me.

His stores were often located in rough neighborhoods. In order not to get robbed, he had to pay local off-duty policemen to stand guard, with their guns exposed, while my father and his guys loaded or unloaded large vans of merchandise into these warehouse spaces. My father often worked with a man named Garson, and when George was not around because he was working late, Garson would sometimes leave messages with me. I was in junior high school then and dutifully wrote these down on small slips of paper that I put by the telephone in a leather holder so my father would see them when he came home. My mother and I never met Garson. That world— of men and business—mostly was separate from us. When my father came home, sometimes at midnight, my mother usually was already asleep in the bedroom. I would be up watching The Late Show in the living room on the pull-out Castro convertible sofa. George would sit on the edge of the bed and tell me about his day—the business he had tried to accomplish and the difficulties he had encountered. I never knew how to help, but I listened and absorbed.

A child cannot solve adult problems or even understand their consequences. I know that now, but I did not understand that then. And so, I always believed I should or could help. Because there was no one else to consult about these dilemmas, I lived in a strange inversion of reality, believing that my parents had been given to me so that I could care for them. But I am sure I am not the only child, particularly not the only "only child," who has felt such an exaggerated weight of responsibility.

My father's sense of failure—of not achieving at the level he had hoped—has followed me my whole life. He was tormented by the thought that he had not provided well enough for us, had not secured our future as he had hoped. But I never had a sense that he had failed. I may not have understood what it would have meant for him to have greater success, but I did internalize his anxiety about it. Throughout my life, I have never felt my accomplishments to be sufficient and I always have worried that there will not be enough money for the future. And despite how productive it may appear from the outside, at times I too have been concerned that my own life has actually been a failure, that I have not realized my potential as I might have. These recurring anxieties are not unlike his own. I can hear my Russian grandmother, Esther, say, "Georgie cries with two loaves of bread under his arm." I fear she would have said the same about me.

Both he and I were looking for some external manifestation of success, but the forms we chose could not have been more different, at least on the surface. My worlds have always been intellectual, filled with communities of artists, writers, activists, and other thinkers trying to find meaning in images, language, ideas, society, and action. His was the world of small, independent businessmen and street people hoping to make a buck. He never could have worked for a boss or filled out time sheets or taken orders for very long. Like him, I am able to negotiate bureaucracy, even to manage it pretty well, but if a job impinges on my principles or on my freedom to think creatively or restrains me from expressing myself as I feel I should, I am always prepared to walk away. It is a kind of internal escape valve that I have cultivated, knowing I can always retreat to something inside myself if necessary, something more powerful and more compelling than the job. I think he was the same.

Although my father worried about our material well-being, I always thought we had everything we needed. I certainly did. But when we would visit his sisters Julia and Sadie, I would observe what we did not have: large living spaces, creamy velour couches, plush white rugs, multiple bedrooms with overstuffed pillows, several bathrooms with bronze sink handles. But these luxuries were as meaningless to me as they were to my mother. The only thing my child-self did wish for, and I wished for it a great deal, was that my mother would have a mink coat, just like my aunts did. It seemed unfair to me that they could have something so glamorous that she did not, especially because she was the one who took care of their parents— my Jewish grandparents—when they were old. When my father's sisters came to visit us in winter, I was often entrusted to take their weighty black and brown mink and sable coats to the bedroom and lay them on the bed. I usually carried them one at a time and placed each with its black silk lining side up, so I could see the flourish of their red embroidered initials stitched on the inside. Sometimes I would fall on top of these coats deliberately or crawl under them to feel their weight. Our apartment did not have a closet wide enough to hang even one. But when I told my mother that I wished she could have such a coat, she shrugged, laughed, and said, "Honey, I don't want a mink coat. I never did. If I had, your father would have bought me one years ago." I did believe that this was how she felt and also knew that my father would have found a way to get her one, nonetheless, it pained me that she had less than my aunts. To me the coat would have been a reward, one she did not desire but deserved.

Perhaps my mother, who had lived on a farm, knew too much about minks to want the pelts of these dead creatures draped across her body. After the mines closed in Hastings in the 1950s, many miners stayed in town and raised minks and sables to earn a living. It always upset me to watch these sleek, frenetic, ferret-like creatures miserably trapped. Confined to cages for their entire short lives, desperate to get out, these animals, pacing back and forth in repetitive movements, would become vicious. They were fed from metal slop buckets full of fish heads to make their fur glossy—a thick, gray mixture with a sickening smell. The men, wearing heavy steel-threaded gloves just in case the minks lunged at them, lowered the food into the cages through small, hinged, trapdoors on top. Minks are like weasels, from the same family but bigger. A sable is a cross between a weasel and a mink, valuable for their extremely sleek coats. But their piercingly sharp teeth can easily cut through a wrist or an anklebone. Whenever one of these creatures escaped in Hastings the town sounded an alarm to alert everyone to stay out of the tall grass.

PINTCHIK'S HARDWARE

My father's business card read: "George Becker, Auctioneer, Liquidator and Appraiser." The logistics of the liquidation business were somewhat elusive to me, but the appraiser part was even more so. As I understood it, my father simply had a particular gift. Coupled with real knowledge of costs and innate mathematical ability, he was able to make appraising part of his daily work and income. He could walk up and down the aisles of a hardware or dry goods store, assess the merchandise on the shelves— quantity and cost—and in a few hours "appraise" the worth of the stock, coming so close to the actual value that the owners would not have to close the shop for a day or two to do a full inventory.

I seem to have inherited this odd skill. Whereas my father really did have an aptitude for numbers, and I am challenged to calculate even the most basic equations, nonetheless I can intuitively guess the expense of a project, even a large-scale one, such as the renovation of a building, within a very close margin of the final cost. I can do this not because I am deeply knowledgeable about such things—not at all—but because the numbers appear to float in front of me magically, as if I only need to grab them from the air and tether them to the ground. My mother and her mother were often thought to be intuitive and even psychic, my father, the last person ever to imagine himself in that way, had a touch of this innate ability as well.

I never really understood the inner workings of my father's business, but at times I did get to see a bit of the process, observing him buy up "stocks" or "dry goods" that individuals and stores wanted to sell, negotiate the "deals," and then resell the merchandise in bulk. People would hear about my father through others or find him in the phone directory listings known as the *Yellow Pages*, which, during that pre-Internet time, was the best way to advertise or to find businesses, or even doctors, you might be looking for. Because my father never did have a permanent office and because there were no cell phones at that time, when someone wanted to reach him, they called our home. At times the calls were about real merchandise worth his effort to assess; other calls were about nothing much or goods that had no bill of sale and therefore were illegal or "hot," which he was clear he, "would not touch." Every now and then on a weekend, when he was going out on a call, he would invite me to join him. During these expeditions I would briefly drop into his world of men, merchandise, and negotiations—thrilled to have a glimpse of it all, and excited to spend time alone with him.

One Saturday morning, when I must have been about

twelve, a man called to say that he had multiple rolls of linoleum stored in the basement of Pintchik's Hardware, a well-known (and still flourishing) landmark store on Bergen Street in Park Slope, Brooklyn. The person who called told my father that the "price would be right." So, we went.

Two men met us outside Pintchik's, where they were renting space from the store to warehouse their linoleum. They led us down a wooden staircase into a low-ceilinged, barely-lit basement. Along the far wall, lined up close to each other stood fifty or more tall rolls of patterned and speckled linoleum (fashionable at the time), spanning almost the entire length of the room. But something about this display must have alerted my father, because as one of the guys was telling him about the many feet of linoleum folded into each roll, my father kept saying, "uh-huh, uh-huh," in a tone that let me know he was only pretending to listen. But he let the guy keep talking, then said, "Honey, go stand against the wall next to that first roll of linoleum and face me." I did not know what he was up to, but I did know he had a plan. My father then came over to adjust my position so that the edge of my shoulder touched the first roll of linoleum towering above me. Then, he shoved me slightly, so that I lost balance and leaned into that first roll, almost falling over it entirely. The rolls soon began cascading into each other, collapsing quickly and noisily in a domino effect, smashing onto the floor. I stood transfixed as the men began to yell at my father. "What the hell did you do?" My father, just shaking his head and smiling, a cigarette in his mouth, said to me, "Come on honey, let's get away from these crooks." The linoleum rolls were still crashing as we walked up out of the basement and onto the street. In the car my father told me that as soon as he saw the linoleum, he knew that the rolls were mostly hollow, which is why they so easily came tumbling down. For my father, a performative gesture was always worth more than any verbal confrontation. It was fun to be his co-conspirator. He was fearless, and when we were together, so was I.

Many years later, when I was already living in Chicago and my parents were still in East Flatbush, my younger cousin Kenny, an investment banker at that time, would often visit my parents in Brooklyn. Kenny's close friend, Morty, then a producer for *Late Night with David Letterman*, had been over to our house with Kenny several times and had observed my father's innate humor and theatricality. One time when Morty was there visiting, my father bumped into the kitchen wall and, unflustered, admonished my mother: "Helen, who the hell put that wall there?" Morty used to say, "I'd love to get George behind the curtain on the Letterman show and then let him try to find his way out. When he did get untangled, whatever he'd say would be hilarious." George was unimpressed by star status, but he would have enjoyed the attention, and it would have made a great story to tell his friends.

When George returned from the war, he went into

business with my uncle Hymie (Herman, actually). But Hymie had serious arthritis and gout, both of which he inherited from the Citrons—my Russian-Jewish grandmother's family. These ailments also plagued my great-uncles Max and Sam, who each had to slice open the sides of their leather shoes to make room for their chronically swollen feet. Hymie was gap-toothed, a bit overweight, wore wire-framed glasses, and radiated kindness. He had never married and, sadly, did not have a family of his own. My mother believed that because he knew he was not well, he never wanted to become a burden to anyone. Because he was alone, my cousins, his nieces, Eleanor and Roberta and I were very important to him, and he was sure to spend time with us. He would have made a wonderful parent and, in fact, became a second father to me.

My uncle enjoyed eating well and knew most of the good restaurants in the city and in upstate New York. He often invited me to accompany him to dinners, and I always dressed for these occasions, wearing short, white gloves and a favorite dress. We often ate at Peter Luger Steak House. "Peter Luger's," as we knew it then and to this day, has heavy wooden tables, no tablecloths, and a cash only policy. As you enter, you can still see the glass cage where a woman counts stacks of money on a tabletop. My uncle and I ate big medium-rare steaks, thick lamb chops, and baked potatoes with lots of butter, sour cream, and chives. We also frequented a restaurant in an old inn near

Bear Mountain. At the entrance of that high-ceilinged, wooden structure was a collection of antique dolls in chintz dresses, "asleep" in small, turn-of-the-century baby carriages. On end tables throughout the lobby, the restaurant had bowls of potpourri that filled the air with too much sweetness, which always made me sneeze.

I have no idea what my uncle and I talked about at those dinners or in the car rides there and back. What could have been interesting to him about the stories or aspirations of a young girl? But I truly enjoyed being with him and he seemed to enjoy being with me. When I was not quite ten years old, my uncle began to have painful, terrible headaches. If he came to visit us in our apartment in the evenings on his way home from work, I had to shut off the television or radio, which annoyed me at the time, but I did not yet understand that he had an inoperable brain tumor, which caused unceasing pounding in his head. He simply could not tolerate noise of any kind. I was too young then to imagine what such suffering could be.

Months later, when my uncle was in the hospital dying, my father sneaked me into the Intensive Care Unit. At that time, I was underage for visiting, but breaking rules never worried my father. He knew how important this visit would be for me and for my uncle; he understood how close we were. I can see myself as I was then: wearing my favorite turquoise V-neck sweater and light-brown corduroy pants, with my hair pulled back in a long ponytail, George and I conspiring how to get me up the stairwell from the lobby unnoticed. But when we reached the top landing, my father put his hand on my shoulder to stop me from going farther and said, "Don't be afraid when you see your uncle. He is getting the best care possible and is not in pain."

When I entered the room, I understood what there was to fear. My uncle was lying flat on a hospital bed, hooked up to several machines. He and the bed were encased in a heavy, large, plastic, transparent oxygen tent—the best technology at that time. The tent was contracting and expanding so that it appeared my uncle was breathing inside a large plastic bag. I could hear the strain on his lungs even through the low-pitched moan of the generator. He was not wearing his glasses, so he could barely see who entered the room. My father pulled a small wooden chair up close to the tent for me. I slid my arm under the plastic curtain and took my uncle's very cold hand and began talking to him, telling him I can no longer remember what. I was crying because it was very clear to me that I might never be with him again. I did not ever want to leave. But my father had a sense of what was enough—for my uncle and for me—so at some point he said that it was time for us to go, before "we got caught." As I suspected, this was my last visit with my uncle. My parents would not let me go to the funeral. They knew I would be too emotional. After he died, I prayed for him every night for years. I asked whoever might be listening from the other side to treat him well and to feed him well. He was always in my consciousness. His death came only one year after that of my grandmother Esther and two years after my grandmother Catherine. By the time I was ten, I had lost three of my most beloved people. I only understood later how powerful these losses must have been for me then.

Hymie was my father's favorite and closest brother. Therefore, his death was also very difficult for George, who soon began to have painful, unrelenting headaches like my uncle's. My mother believed they were a reaction to the sadness of loss, because my father, unlike my mother and me, was unable to cry. Through various business connections, George had met and befriended Peter Bove, the then Comptroller of the Virgin Islands. He invited my father and Larry, my father's lawyer friend, to visit him for a long weekend. (Larry definitely drank too much but to me he was heroic, because he could do the New York Times crossword puzzle in ink.) My mother and I encouraged my father to go with Larry, and we were right to do so. George returned rested and brought me back a tourist set of small wooden bongo drums that had a painted palm tree in green at the base and "Virgin Islands" written in red script right below that. After the trip, my father's headaches stopped. Later we learned that the doctors had thought he might have had glaucoma.

When my uncle died, he left me ten thousand dollars, which remained in an account in the Williamsburg Savings Bank (across from Peter Luger's) until I withdrew it decades later to live on while writing my first book.

HASTINGS

My father shared my love for the urban life and also my deep closeness to many of the people in his family. But he did not really share my other life—the Pennsylvania world of my mother's Polish Catholic mining family. It is easy to identify me as a Russian-Jewish New Yorker by my appearance, accent, and urbanity. But that is only half the story. I was also raised by my agrarian, Polish Catholic family, whose influence perhaps is not as apparent but was nonetheless formative. The rural experiences of my childhood gave me a sense that class was complex and that my dual identity was as well. Summers and sometimes winter breaks in Pennsylvania taught me that nature was bountiful and calming and also a great antidote to the intensity and density of our New York City life. It also taught me that there were multiple bodies of knowledge that my Polish relatives had mastered about the farm, its animals, and its demands, knowledge that I valued and that they were willing to share.

Each summer of my childhood, right after school ended in late June, my mother and I would take the overnight train from the old, magnificent Penn Station in Manhattan to Altoona, Pennsylvania. We always reserved a Pullman sleeper and ate dinner in the dining car, which, in those days, had white tablecloths and actual porcelain plates and silverware. Because we were only two for dinner, the waiters asked that we sit with other guests at the immovable tables designed for four. As I had done with my uncle, I always wore dresses and white gloves to these dinners and enjoyed the conversations with strangers. I also loved the Pullman car, with its miniature bathroom and sink. It was as if we had moved into a dollhouse for a night, put to sleep by the rhythm of the train rattling west. After a winter in our tiny Brooklyn apartment, there was always a sense of impending freedom waiting in the Allegheny Mountains and, of course, great excitement to see my Polish family. My cousin Cindy came from Chicago, and my cousin Essie and I from Brooklyn. Our cousins Vince and Barbara lived on the farm in Hastings with their parents.

My anticipation of the journey was so great that my parents refused to tell me until the night before when my mother and I would be leaving; otherwise, I would have been unable to sleep. The trip took sixteen hours, if all went well. Once we arrived in Altoona, my uncle Jakie would pick us up in his light-gray Buick, which had a darker-gray velour interior, and we would head for Hastings. We stayed on the farm until the end of August, while my father, to my great sadness, remained in Brooklyn, working in the sticky, sooty, unbearably hot, and now, for him, also lonely city.

I imagined him home alone at night in the apartment, the two large, box-shaped floor fans vibrating against the linoleum, the snake plants balanced on saucers with little pools of water at their bases, and my sweet potato plants, with their abundant green leaves dangling almost to the ground—all left on the kitchen sink so he would not forget to water them. Next to the plants, we piled cans of cat food with an opener so he would not forget to feed Cyrano. I imagined George hunched over the small Formica kitchen table, eating canned sardines in olive oil with saltine crackers for dinner, followed by a big slice of watermelon, which he always ate with a knife and fork—tired, sweaty, and shirtless in his madras-plaid Bermuda shorts that revealed his long, remarkably milky-white legs, unable to sleep although exhausted from the heat, probably staying up late watching *Gunsmoke* reruns on television, perhaps unsettled because we were not there.

When my uncle Jakie still worked in the Hastings mines, my cousins and I would sometimes bring his lunch to him at the entrance of the mine shaft closest to my grandmother's house. But after the mines closed in the 1950s, with no work for him or other miners, all my uncles left Pennsylvania to find employment at Swift Foods in the stockyards of Chicago, in repair shops in New York City, and in the automobile industry in Cleveland. Like my father, my uncles Lou and John, working in these locations during the summers, only visited once when they could get away. My uncle Jakie and his family had returned to Hastings to take care of my grandmother, but Jakie now had to travel to Ohio each week to work at General Motors. So, while the men stayed in the cities, the women and children spent July and August together in Pennsylvania.

In part, the children were rushed to "the country" to escape the risk of polio, which was rampant in the United States during the 1950s. My mother and my Polish relatives also believed that the next generation—we who did not have to leave school to work in the mines, plow the fields, feed the pigs, or bail the hay, who had plenty to eat and shoes to wear, for whom they had worked so hard—should also have a real childhood in the country—all summer long. And so, we did. Cindy, Vince, and I were the same age and roamed the hills of the Smokey Valley together. Essie and Barbara, a few years older and mostly unwilling to play with us anymore, nonetheless had each other. Our mothers packed lunches for us every morning, and we did not return to the farm until late afternoon. No one worried about our safety. We drank sweet spring water that rolled across rocks covered in green moss. We ate wild gooseberries, blackberries, black raspberries, red raspberries, blueberries, huckleberries, and elderberries, until our hands and faces were stained purple. Together with our mothers and aunts (and Bennie, our dog), we picked enough berries to bake cobblers and muffins most days and to make jam preserves and dried fruit for the winter. When together like this, we did not return from these mountain excursions until all our coffee-can buckets were filled.

When the weather was hot, we swam in a shallow creek that was a road and a pasture away from my grandmother's house. Our uncles taught us that if we wanted to deepen the creek's water enough to actually swim in it, we had to build a dam. Each year, often with their help, we dug out the creek bed with shovels and then reinforced the banks with rocks from the creek's bottom and with sod that grew on its edges. Wasps loved to settle into the wet clay banks, and each year, at our peril, we chose to disturb these nests just enough to cover our entire bodies with that thick gray-blue ooze, letting the clay dry in the sun until our faces were so taut that we could barely speak. Then we would plunge into the cool, orange water to wash it off.

It never occurred to us to worry that this Kool-Aid–colored creek that turned our swimsuits orange was filled with runoff sulfur, iron, and chemicals from the mines that might be dangerous to our health. In those days, no one in the family ever talked about the toxicity of the mining industry—not even after my grandmother died from ovarian cancer and my uncle Lou developed black lung disease from his time as a child miner. Like everyone in the town, the men were just happy to have work for as long as it lasted; they feared being upended from their homes and lives when it disappeared. There were orange creeks and narrow orange rivers all over western Pennsylvania at that time. They were actually a source of local pride because they signaled to outsiders that the town was prosperous—mines were close by and men had jobs. There were also bony piles throughout Hastings, made up of accumulated waste material from the mining process—shale and carboniferous sandstone—that the companies never bothered to remove. As children, we rode imaginary horses up and down those piles, sometimes tripping and lacerating our knees on the black and gray porous stones, which resembled volcanic rock. There was enough compressed coal in the mix that sometimes these mounds would catch fire and light up the night with rainbow colors and, as I now understand, also emit toxic pollution and greenhouse gases.

My urban cousins and I were always aware that we were more privileged than the farm boys and girls whose chores never ended and who could only join us at the creek at the end of their workday, if at all. Many of them had their own "pools" on the farm—deep, wide holes clawed out with bulldozers. But these were sad looking, more like drainage ditches filled with well water and rainwater, than actual pools. They had muddy bottoms and were stark on the landscape with no grass or trees surrounding them. The "farm kids" happily plunged into the water anyway and floated on tire inner tubes when their work was done. We were "city kids" who came to Hastings for vacation during the summer months and, because of that, we were also of another class, although financially just a bit above their situation. Still, we were different: more savvy about the world outside Hastings, better educated as a result of the superior public schools we attended and because we were able to stay in school rather than leave to work on the farm. We understood that we would have more options than the farm kids ever would, but they knew so much that we wanted to learn: how to milk cows, birth a calf, drive a tractor, plow a field, build a fence, bail hay, and dig a well. I am sure those kids would have loved to have days free to roam and invent games. Theirs was the life my mother and her siblings had inherited, but left behind when the mines closed. To us they seemed very capable and responsible and, in that sense, much beyond us in maturity. We admired them, but we understood that they had to grow up fast—the farms and their families depended on it. My cousins and I were encouraged to be children for as long as we could.

Once a summer, my father would visit Hastings. He was not one to sit overnight on a train and rarely one to drive alone from New York City if he did not have to. He would usually take a turboprop plane from New York into the small Altoona airport where my uncle Jakie would pick him up and drive him to the farm. He always brought a bit of the city with him, wearing a short-sleeve shirt and an open suit jacket with a mix of sweat and Old Spice aftershave, that reminded me of our New York life. But once in Hastings, worn out from working throughout the summer and now in the country with "all that quiet," he would mostly sleep.

My mother's brothers loved to recount George's first visit to Hastings. My parents were returning from seeing relatives with my aunt and uncle. Jakie was driving and my parents were in the backseat. It was late in the evening and dark outside when, while passing some fields, my mother exclaimed, "The radishes are coming up." To which my father replied, "How the hell can you see that in the dark?" But my mother was not referring to a new crop of vegetables peeking out of the ground, but rather to the radishes she ate at dinner, that were now "coming up" again, as heartburn.

My parents, clearly, responded to the "country" in different ways. When in Hastings, my mother was returning to her original home and was completely comfortable. As soon as we arrived, she took off her shoes and never put them on again except when we headed for town or to the train back to the city. My father, from Williamsburg, Brooklyn, somewhat lost in this rural environment, often asked, "What the hell do people do here?" Given all the time he had already spent in Hastings with my mother, my grandmother and the rest of her family, it is surprising that the farm always remained so alien to him.

There are photos of my parents, before I was born, standing near the family farmhouse, with the tavern in the background, relaxed, smiling, my mother tall and fashionable in Katherine Hepburn–style wide, loose-fitting pants, her hair swept up in a chignon, my father slouching, taller than her but not by much, his arm draped across her neck. In another, my father is kneeling and holding up my infant self in front of him, showing me off to the camera, like a prize. I was dressed in a long, white, lace garment, perhaps for my baptism. Because my Catholic mother feared that if I became ill and died, without being baptized, I would go to purgatory, my father had agreed to it. I doubt he understood my mother's anxiety and surely the concept did not have enough meaning for him to object, so it took place in Pennsylvania.

Although I greatly anticipated my father's visits, I cannot reconstruct much about them. But I do remember that one time my uncles must have taken George to another farm to buy some baby rabbits as a surprise for me. I was thrilled to have three very small bunnies to care for—black, white, and gray. But catastrophe befell the most adorable white one when I took her with me to the outhouse where there were two open-hole seats, which my cousins and I sometimes shared with each other or with our mothers. While I sat on one, I put the bunny down on the wooden separator between the openings, but the bunny moved too quickly and fell into the other hole. I was screaming as my white bunny was drowning in all that slop. I immediately ran outside. My uncle heard me and came running. He tried to save her by knocking over the outhouse, but he must already have known that, as small as she was, she really never had a chance.

I was twelve the summer my father actually drove to Hastings himself to take us to the Grand Canyon. I had been looking forward to the trip for months, reading all I could about it in my *World Book Encyclopedia*. The plan was that he would pick us up in Hastings and we would leave directly from there together and head west. Given how much my father hated to drive and loved to stop "under every tree," as my mother would say, we estimated the journey would take a week. But when my father arrived at the farm, he said he needed to talk with me. We sat outside on small stools in the grass behind the house and there he told me that we would not be able to go on the trip because he was in the middle of "lotting up" a big stock of goods in New York and could not get away for that long. I saw clearly that he was having great difficulty telling me this. I must have cried, which doubtless pained him enormously. He drove all that way from New York just to tell me this in person, dreading how disappointed I surely would be.

My father was devoted to us. Of this I was certain then and am certain now, but he was always working and thus often absent from our lives. It was not uncommon in those days for husbands to work nights and weekends, leaving their wives to care for the children. So, the expectation of planned or unplanned time with him had great meaning for me. Like my father with his restless spirit, I was also always ready to set out, and I could become inconsolable, and sometimes even angry when the possibility of an adventure was taken away from me. I am the same to this day, although I am mostly better able to hide my disappointments and even let the sadness go, when I need to.

POINT PLEASANT BEACH

Some years after my Polish grandmother died, and my aunt Helen and uncle Jakie moved permanently to Cleveland, we stopped going to the farm for the summers. Instead, my mother and I began spending time with my father in Point Pleasant Beach, New Jersey, where he had been running the auction room on the Boardwalk for some years. Because we had always been away for the summers, we were unknown to his New Jersey friends, business partners, and coworkers. In Point Pleasant, we finally met Irving Block, someone I had been taking phone messages from for years.

Irving was my father's closest friend, an adorable man with curly brown hair. He was short, always in khaki pants, a light-blue button-down shirt, a darker-blue golfing jacket, and what in those days we called "tennis shoes." He also drove an old, beige station wagon with wooden side panels and was completely unpretentious, although he had "studied business at Harvard," a place that seemed impossibly far away and impressive to us. He was also extremely wealthy, having inherited a big expanse of boardwalk real estate at Point Pleasant Beach from his father. When my mother and I met him for the first time, Irving said teasingly that he had always thought there might be something "wrong or odd" about us because my father had never brought us to New Jersey before. My mother and I became close to Irving and to his wife,

Rose, and also to Rose's Italian parents, the Cinellis. In late fall and winter, when the Boardwalk was shut down, we would often spend weekends with them in their small, brick house in Deal, New Jersey.

My mother and I loved Rose's mother, Mrs. Cinelli, as we always called her. Like many older Italian women, she wore black and went to church each morning, as if she were still living in an Italian village. Rose and she were always repairing or sewing dresses and skirts for themselves and others. Mrs. Cinelli had a gentleness in her face and in her voice, as did her daughter. They were northern Italian and both had very fair, almost translucent skin, which made their small, blue veins apparent. Mrs. Cinelli's husband, Frank—Mr. Cinelli to us—had retired from the post office and spent a great deal of time in his basement workshop making wooden birdhouses and mailboxes for friends and family. They often returned to their village of Ivrea, Italy, where Olivetti had a big plant, to visit and to help their family financially as they could.

One Christmas when I was twelve years old, Rose gave me an Italian, twenty-carat-gold charm bracelet. Every year after that, she added another miniature charm—small dice in a woven gold cage, a cat with an emerald eye, a bicycle with a diamond and ruby in the spokes, a miniature Ferris wheel with moveable seats. It was wondrous to me that such tiny things could be made so elegantly and brought to me from Italy. The Blocks had never had children, so they were extremely kind to me and also to their niece Pamela, who had what I thought to be the most fashionable wardrobe. She was probably five years older than I, and everything she wore I wished I owned. Eventually some of those garments did make their way to me—a patterned, cream, bodice-shirred dress with dark-green velvet trim and a bouffant skirt, for one. I wore that dress to many Bar Mitzvahs, teasing my hair to match the bell shape of the skirt and dying my shoes the same color as the green trim, all very au courant in Brooklyn at the time.

The auction room that brought us all to Point Pleasant Beach was a marginal affair: a large space filled with wood-slatted folding chairs and a dark-brown, faux-wood, linoleum floor. It had the sparse look of a church basement. On one side of the room, the doors slid open to the Boardwalk, with its endless parade of day-trippers heading for or leaving the beach, and beyond it the ocean and horizon. There were many such auction rooms in Jersey beach towns in those days. They were places where people could come in from the sun or the rain and maybe take home a treasure or bargain. George hired Phil King "to work the block" and do the actual auctioneering. Phil—whom my father called a "Limey"—had a British accent, which gave him some "European" authority when he did the pitch to sell "Intercontinental Geneva" watches (that had nothing to do with Switzerland), to sunburnt tourists. The auction room must have paid off financially because my father spent many summers running that operation, accumulating merchandise from his stocks during the year to keep it going. I am certain Irving gave him a good rental price for the room to make sure that my father would make a profit each year.

Now, almost a teenager, I worked on the Boardwalk next door to the auction room making fudge in the candy shop run by Phil's very large wife, Bertha, whom my father unkindly referred to, in private at least, as "Battleship Bertha." She then also "hired" me to pour the waffle mix onto the griddle and make the endless stacks needed for the ice cream sandwiches we sold throughout the day. After I piled up enough waffles, my next job was to move the ice cream bricks—striped with vanilla, chocolate, and strawberry—from the freezer, unwrap the paper from each one and place one brick between two waffles. I would then wrap the ice cream sandwiches in waxed brown paper, hand them to the customers, and take the cash. I also eventually was tasked with keeping the saltwater taffy machine running all day. These summer jobs lasted until I started going to sleepaway camp at age fourteen. I do not remember ever getting paid for my labor at Bertha's, but since my father was working hard, I wanted to be useful, too. And there were perks. As part of the Boardwalk crew and known to other workers there as a fellow employee, I was invited to ride free on the Bubble Bounce and Twister—and although I was underage, I was also allowed to drive the go-karts.

I am not sure what my mother did while my father and

I both were working. She was never one for sitting on the beach. There was no swimming at Point Pleasant Beach most of the time anyway because the surf was usually too rough. Ropes were attached to poles set deep into the coarse sand so that people could hang onto them and not get swept away by the strong undertow at the shoreline. Maybe my mother read novels or talked to Babe, who owned and ran the rooming house where we always stayed, right beyond the Boardwalk. I am sure she cooked our meals. Although my mother always adapted to circumstances and did not complain, she must have been lonely in Point Pleasant, after all those summers on the farm surrounded by her mother, sisters-in-laws, nieces, nephews, neighbors, and, for most years, her visiting brothers—all living together in her family home. She must have missed the animals as well, and the garden. She had not yet learned to drive and perhaps longed for some autonomy.

But I loved those Jersey Shore summers. They gave me a true appreciation for beach resorts, carnies, and working on holidays. In my late twenties and into my thirties, while writing my first book, I bartended at several Chicago neighborhood bars—jazz and blues clubs mostly. I particularly liked to work on New Year's Eve when other people were out on dates or partying. I always made great tips on those occasions and sometimes received unexpected gifts, which I saved to return to the customers who, the next day, when sober, would invariably return to reclaim their expensive rings or the hundred-dollar bills they had forced on me in their drunken, holiday exuberance. But my preference for working while others played, surely came from those days on the Boardwalk and the camaraderie I felt with my fellow workers then. I also learned to see no work as beneath me. Even when I was older, with a career as a professor and head of the graduate program at the School of the Art Institute of Chicago, I always took note of the signs posted at the Marshall Field department store window, advertising part-time retail jobs during the Christmas season. And although I never actually applied for these jobs, it was reassuring to me that, if I were ever short of cash, there would always be part-time work I could do or a bar that needed tending. Of course, at some point, I had to leave this type of work behind, the rest of my life and my new professional "status" having caught up with me.

Still, I was always particularly comfortable working in bars and clubs, having spent many summer days in Hastings visiting my mother and aunts in the tavern next to my grandmother's house, which they took turns running. My uncles had built the tavern for my grandmother before they left for World War II when they anticipated that she would need a source of income. They also knew a tavern would not lose money because coal miners always stopped for one beer or more on their way home each night. When the miners ordered a shot and a beer, they usually poured the shot into the beer (what we, on the Northside of Chicago, called a "boiler maker"). The tavern was a dark place that always smelled rancid—the very distinct odor of beer seeped into every crevice. My uncles had designed and built a simple structure that suited the miners and the community best: a dark, cavernous space with a long, wooden bar and another huge room for parties and Polish weddings, that often lasted for days.

In my experience, the Jersey Shore was about commerce. Irving Block's "Rip Tide Bar" was always packed with tourists. A glass of beer cost twenty-five cents, and people drank until they fell down. When the bar closed at midnight, we would drive north—my father, Irving, the bartender, and I—to an all-night deli in Asbury Park. My mother must have gone to bed early, because I don't remember her accompanying us on any of these escapades. Nor did she seem to worry about me, even though I was out late, because she knew I was with my father.

During these midnight escapades, the talk between George and his friends was all about money—business successes, failures, and possibilities. We sat in the deli's Naugahyde booths until 2 a.m., paper bags filled with cash from Irving's bar till stashed between us. We ate pastrami sandwiches on rye bread so stuffed with greasy, spicy meat that you could hardly fit them in your mouth. There were times when Irving forgot the bags and only realized he had left the money once we landed in Point Pleasant, and then we would have to turn the car around, drive back and pick them up. They were usually still there between the sectionals, where we had left them or near the register where the owner had stashed them while awaiting our return. They all knew Irving well and liked him a great deal for his kindness and even for his forgetfulness.

Although I was on my way to becoming a scholar of sorts, immersed in novels, beat poetry, and ideas, I loved knowing how things worked or did not work in the more material world. In those Jersey Shore days, I was a "night owl," like my father, and always up for any excursion. Those late-night forays with George, Irving, and their friends gave me confidence to move in the world of men. I was often in the role of my father's sidekick and, as such, I felt we understood each other and enjoyed each other. I also was very protective of him. I defended him against my mother, my aunts, and anyone else who attempted to deride, diminish, or disparage him, however good-natured or harmless their intentions.

From time to time, my mother would talk about how distracted my father seemed and how inept he was at fixing things and navigating geography, tasks at which she excelled. She would tell humorous stories about him, but at his expense. One such was about our car trip upstate when we stayed at a motel on a small lake and my father offered to row me to the other side. I was surprised that George knew how to row at all and that he wanted to do such an athletic activity, so I was excited to go out with him. In the morning, he was already in the boat when I got to the pier. I had just put one foot into the hull and was about to put in the other, when my father began rowing away. It was not such a big deal to me when I fell in the water—I could swim and I could swim in lakes—but to my mother this incident exemplified my father's obliviousness to the physical world. She told another story about his poor sense of direction, or the absence of a sense of direction (a limitation I also share). In the late 1950s, when we were in New York during the summer months, we would go to the Acquacades on Long Island, a fabulous holdover from the 1939 New York World's Fair, to see a theatrical production of synchronized swimming. The stadium housed thousands of people, who all parked their cars in the same large lot. But, when we came out, my father never could remember where he had parked the car. Invariably, we would have to wait until most or all of the other cars had left, to finally locate ours.

These were innocent and humorous stories, but it hurt me that my mother would expose actions that made my father look foolish. He, of course, was not bothered by any of this—always confident in everyone's affection for him, he also could laugh at himself. Teasing or complaining about the men of the family was pervasive among my Jewish aunts who often made fun of my uncles—their awkwardness, obsessions, inadequacies, eccentricities, and habits. I never doubted that my aunts loved these men and were devoted to them. I knew they were grateful for how hard their husbands worked for their families. So why deride them if they fell asleep at dinner, before dinner, or lost themselves in television, or ate too much? Clearly, they were exhausted and needed diversion. My aunts' behavior sometimes bordered on contempt for the men they had married, but perhaps this kind of storytelling or teasing was just how these relationships had evolved. The tables turned the other way as well in Borscht-belt, Catskill humor when male comedians performed endless shticks about their families and their marriages, making fun of and calling out their wives and mothers-in-law. This behavior troubled me. Why would you demean someone you loved? These seemingly inevitable small betrayals made me think that I would never marry. I vowed to myself that I surely would not humiliate any of the men in my life or allow myself to be humiliated by them. But, as it turned out, I would have little control over any of that.

PART III:
TO DISOWN

*F*reud's 1913 book <u>Totem and Taboo</u>, presents his theory of the myth of the primal horde. In this fantastical imagining of the beginnings of civilization and guilt, the originary family lives in close proximity to each other, under the strict rule of the patriarch/father. When the grown sons tire of the father's dominance and restrictions, especially those controlling sexual access to the mother and sisters, they plot to kill the father.

After performing this murderous act, the sons consume the father's body to symbolically ingest his weight and assume their place in the hierarchy, but they soon understand the magnitude of their actions and experience remorse. To assuage their guilt, they begin to worship the father as a totem. In time they recognize that their own sons are now beginning to plot their demise, with the intent of using equally bloody tactics to usurp their power. It is then that they enact laws to prohibit patricide.

Although the women of the family are central to this drama as objects of desire, they have neither agency nor voice. Does the mother really want to become the concubine of her most powerful son? Are the daughters easily resigned to becoming the wives of their brothers? Freud does not concern himself with their potential reactions. Whereas a son's journey is here mythically envisioned, no such archetypes are presented for a daughter, whose path to maturity and whose place in social structures remain uncharted. The daughter may become a concubine and/or a mother, but if she does not also gain *power in the public sphere, she cannot transcend the law of the father or be free to develop her own life's narrative. To have access to such autonomy and self-definition, she must oppose the law of the patriarch, but if she dares, there will be consequences.*

ADOLESCENCE

I adored George. He was the prototype/archetype for all the glamorous, charismatic, handsome men to follow in my life. In them I often found his theatricality, excitement, and playfulness, but I did not find the devotion and loyalty that he exhibited to me and my mother. I did not even understand to look for those qualities or to value them until much later. As a result, during my twenties and thirties, my life was constantly upended by my personal relationships with fabulously narcissistic men.

During my early childhood, George did not seem to recognize that he was raising a girl and not a boy, a girl whose life one day would be filled with adventures that might threaten him and with men of whom he might not approve. I doubt he had thought much about the reality that his daughter, always encouraged to be confident in her judgment of the world, would one day refuse to back down even to him and would always insist on choosing her own path. Nor had he anticipated that, having spent so much time with him and having observed my extremely self-assured mother, I would always assume my equality as I negotiated the world of men.

As I grew older, this early permission to be strong created enormous conflict between my father and me. He repeatedly challenged my confidence in my own judgment with his irrational fear that I could end up a "loose" woman or destroy my "reputation"—concepts often repeated to girls in the 1950s. I have always believed that my father was traumatized when my cousin Eleanor, ten years my senior, became pregnant as a teenager. She once told me that my father (acting as the patriarch of the family) and our mutually adored Uncle Hymie had been very cruel to her when she became pregnant, calling her terrible names. They had then pressured Eleanor to marry her Italian Catholic boyfriend. I was shocked to learn this, but I was already aware that her "situation" was considered a tragedy at that time. Although I never felt Eleanor was unhappy, even when she and her husband had to rely on her parents for financial support. She had a joyful spirit and a biting, sarcastic humor, like her mother, my aunt Harriet. But my Jewish family must have shamed and ostracized her to such an extent that she and her husband never attended large family events, such as Bar Mitzvahs, Passover dinners, or weddings. The perception was not only that she had married outside her religion (just as my parents had done), but that she had married beneath her class, although her parents, like mine, were not even middle class in terms of material wealth or education.

Nonetheless the family looked down on her husband, who was a truck driver and whom they thought unworthy of her. I heard my father say, more than once, that Eleanor had "ruined her life."

My first direct encounter with my father's capacity for irrational and cruel behavior toward me occurred when I was in fifth grade. Some neighbor from our apartment building must have told my mother that they saw me, far from our block, after school, walking with a group of boys and girls close to where one of my male classmates lived. The boys were friends from school, not boys I had picked up on the street. But my mother repeated what the neighbor told her to my father and, that evening, my father confronted me. I was astounded by his irate, accusatory tone, his disproportionate rage because I had been walking with boys he did not know. I had never experienced such coldness from him, and, for the first time ever, he frightened me. "What were you doing with those boys? Who were they? Why were you so far from our neighborhood?" Even then, I understood that this inquiry had something to do with sex, but at that time, all our friends ever did together was play spin the bottle—which we might have been planning to do that day, I can no longer remember—but the implicit accusation was that something truly tawdry had occurred. I was in shock. I know I was in tears.

My mother was very angry at my father's excessive response and perhaps she too was horrified to see him railing at me in this way. She finally confronted him and said, "Do you think all boys are as wild as you were when you were young?" In the midst of this scene, I could feel myself leave my body and retreat into a kind of detached haze—a response to fear and trauma that I have experienced innumerable times since then. At that moment, I had found a way to disappear inside myself, where I felt safe, albeit lonely.

My father's need to control my relationships with boys and later with men grew even more pronounced. But even this first betrayal—his betrayal of me and my supposed betrayal of him—shaped my resolve that, as much as I loved him, as much as I wanted him to love and respect me, I would never succumb to this behavior. He would not control me, and I would not live my life to please him. Of this I already was certain. Such constraints, ties that bind, felt like death to me. Even at that age, I had ambitions to become educated, to travel, to learn languages, to live bravely, to have relationships with whomever I chose, and to write. But to actualize these desires, I knew I needed to be free and I was surprised to realize that the first man to unseat my equilibrium by trying to keep me from that life was my adored father.

When I was in high school, my father's obsession with the boys I came to know became intolerable for him and for me. I can no longer remember how our fights began. I only know they must have been intense because there were periods when we did not speak to each other for days. To communicate with him during these times, I would leave notes taped to the bathroom mirror in the morning asking him to bring home something I needed from his stores: legal pads, paperclips, or pens. He would then deposit the desired items on the table in the hallway when he returned from work in the evening.

In the middle of one of our most intense arguments—it must have been about how late I could stay out and with whom—my mother collapsed onto the kitchen floor. Fearing she might have had a heart attack, my father and I both dropped down to our knees beside her. The vitriolic timbre of our argument was simply too much for her temperament. When we finally got her up and onto a chair, she said to my father, "You wanted her to be strong and stand up for herself, but when she does, you try to beat her down." This was now the second time I had witnessed my mother defending me to my father, although I suspect she said much more in private.

By 1961, we had moved to Glenwood Road in what was then called East Flatbush but is now known as Midwood Park. My parents had purchased a house that cost fifteen thousand dollars. Although my father avoided debt when he could, he had borrowed the money for the down payment from his dear friend Irving Block. It was a huge sum for George at that time, and he was very eager to pay it back. The house was a three-story Victorian with a large living room, dining room, kitchen, and kitchenette on the first floor, and six bedrooms on the next two floors. It also had a yard. Although beyond luxurious in size and layout for us after our apartment in Crown Heights, it probably was priced as low as it was because it was right next to the above-ground subway, then called the Brighton Line, later the BMT, and now the D, near the Newkirk Avenue stop. Whenever the trains went by, which, except in the middle of the night, was very often, the entire house rattled, especially at rush hour when the trains traveled frequently from Manhattan to Coney Island and back again. It was particularly noisy in the summer months when, before air conditioning, our windows were open to catch a breeze.

In Woody Allen's 1977 film, *Annie Hall*, the narrator insists that his childhood-self grew up in a ramshackle wooden house directly under one of the landmark Coney Island rollercoasters, the Thunderbolt. Whenever the rollercoaster cars plunge down the ridiculously steep, terrifying, rickety, tracks—passengers screaming with fear and joy—the whole house shakes. I know Woody Allen never lived in Coney Island because, like me, he went to Midwood High School and that school district is nowhere near the Thunderbolt. But his image of the raucous, clanging rollercoaster is reminiscent of the whizzing, vibrating subway I actually did live next to for years.

The move to East Flatbush, which was primarily about getting me into a white, middle-class, high school, was also, of course, about having more space. As I got older, it became impossible to live in three rooms on Albany Avenue, without a place where I could study or visit with my friends. With this move, we now had a huge amount of space, more than we would ever need. I also knew that this luxury would be short-lived for me because in three years I would be off to college. As a result, I never did connect deeply with the house or that neighborhood. I never found a sense of community there or rooted my psyche on those streets as I had done in Crown Heights, which now had become the "old neighborhood" for me. I was already focused on my next life in college and being on my own—this move was just a stop along the way.

But the house did allow me to study because, incredibly, I had the entire attic floor to myself. I was able to immerse myself completely in my schoolwork without interruption. During those high school years, I used to do my Latin and French homework with my head under the inflatable hood of a plastic, portable, baby-blue hair dryer—whether I had just washed my hair or not. I did not understand the science of this then, or even wonder why I had better retention when I studied under this helmet of whirling air. I now know that it was the white noise of the machine that actually helped me concentrate and thus more easily memorize those endless French idioms and Latin declensions. I also used this private, third-floor space to listen to jazz and blues records on an old-fashioned hi-fi system, which my father had acquired in one of his stocks. But as perfect as this arrangement might seem, I was lonely, having left my cousins and friends in Crown Heights.

Fortunately, our backyard was adjacent to that of a large, exuberant, Italian American family: the Napolis— Tony, Regina, and their children Susie, Peter, and Linda— who quickly adopted my parents and me, inviting us to all their family events: Sicilian Christmas Eve dinners (The Feast of the Seven Fishes), christenings of nieces and nephews, New Year's Eve parties, weddings, Halloween costume soirées, and cruises to the Bahamas and Bermuda, with their extended family in tow. My father developed a deep friendship with Tony Napoli, who, although still young had served on the police force for twenty-five years. When my mother came home from work at night and did not find George in our house, she would stand on the back porch, where she could see across the yard into the Napoli's kitchen window to check if my father was sitting at their dinette table. She would usually find him there having his first dinner of spaghetti and meatballs with them, as a prelude to his second dinner at our house with us.

When the weather was warm enough, Tony and my father would sit in the backyard in beach chairs talking into the night. When it was really hot, they might stand in our small plastic pool. These 4-foot-high plunge pools with light-blue liners were popular in Brooklyn at the time, where yards were small and full-size swimming pools non-existent. Even while standing in the pool, both men were always smoking—Cuban cigars for Tony and unfiltered Camel cigarettes for my father.

It was odd to move from Crown Heights, a racially diverse, working-class, immigrant, and first-generation neighborhood, which was almost a shtetl, to what was, at that time (although is no longer) a predominantly white, middle-class neighborhood inhabited by Reformed, Orthodox, and secular Jews, as well as some working-class Italian families, like the Napolis.

Midwood High School

Although relocating to East Flatbush offered me a fantastic academic opportunity—an intense language-arts program that prepared me well for college and for much after that—there was no real joy in my high school experience, just an enormous amount of hard work. I could not replicate the deep connections of my Crown Heights extended family and I only really had one good friend, Diana. She and I talked a great deal about the restrictions in our homes and the anticipated launch into the rest of our lives after high school. We each dreamed of Manhattan—only a mile and half across the bridge but another universe, where the chances to explore art, culture, and ideas seemed infinite.

Having made the move to Midwood High School, I leapt out of my socioeconomic class into a world I had experienced a bit while at Camp Lokanda in upstate New York, where I spent summers after I outgrew the Boardwalk life of Point Pleasant Beach. It was there that, for the first time, I really noticed class differences in terms of money, education, and culture. Many of the friends I made at this camp lived in large and what seemed to me at that time very extravagant houses on Long Island. My parents must have saved all year to send me there. But as a result of this experience, our Crown Heights building and apartment then seemed impoverished to me. If I planned to visit my camp friends in the fall, I always tried to meet them in the city, where we could go to a museum or a concert. I was embarrassed to bring them back to my own home and then ashamed at such feelings, as if I were betraying my family and all those I loved.

Now at Midwood, I was surrounded by many students who were from professional families, which increased my sense of inadequacy. Most were extremely smart and, in addition to classes at school, took music and dance lessons, read books I had not yet heard of, and traveled to Aruba and places equally unknown to me for winter break.

In December of my first year at Midwood, a teacher wrote the name "Beethoven" on the blackboard; it was the anniversary of the composer's birth. She then asked what we could tell her about him and his work. Many of the students raised their hands and had a great deal to say. Although hard for me to imagine now, his name was unknown to me then. When I got home, I immediately read his biography in my *World Book Encyclopedia*. Thus, I began a very intense period of attempting to educate myself and to fill in the knowledge of culture that I now understood was surprisingly lacking. I read and studied intensely, just to stay at the same level as my fellow students, many of whom went on to get high SAT scores and were accepted into the most prestigious colleges and universities. I, who tested badly on all national exams, had no such successes and no aspirations for the Ivy League, nor did I really understand what it was. Still, as a result of working very hard, I graduated sixteenth in my class of 1,500 students. I was an enigma to the high school academic counselors, who were certain I must have been unduly distracted on the day of the SAT exams to score as low as I did. But I knew that those types of exams were never going to be my strength. I honestly often did not understand the thinking behind the questions or know what were considered appropriate responses. Even on the reading comprehension parts of those exams, the offered interpretations of the texts seemed imperfect to me. This relationship to tests later carried over to the GRE exams, as well, and I began to accept, remarkably without self-consciousness, that I had a different kind of mind—one I was determined to cultivate.

Although I knew little about classical music, I had fallen in love with opera while living in Crown Heights. The Italian shoemaker down the street was always listening to Puccini while he worked. My mother also loved opera and often had it on the radio as she cooked. By the time I was in my second year of high school, I was frequenting the old Metropolitan Opera's Saturday matinees. I loved going to Manhattan alone and standing with the old Italian men from the boroughs, who were dressed in their long black or brown coats. This low-priced box was just above and to the right of the stage, so we had a perfect view. It only cost a dollar to stand, and it was thrilling to do so, even though we sometimes stood for four hours or more to hear *Faust* or *Aida* (with live elephants on the stage).

In those days, before the opera began, announcers admonished the audience: "Do not throw roses. Do not throw roses." But as soon as the production ended and the audience was up on its feet applauding and cheering, the men near me (who had hummed along throughout the entire performance) would open their coats, where they had pinned long-stemmed roses vertically onto the linings. As the performers took their bows, with "Bravo" reverberating throughout the concert hall, my compatriots with great flourish extended their arms and tossed their roses over the balustrade and onto the stage. It was exhilarating to be with true aficionados— and the most fun I have ever had at the opera. A few years later, when I was in college, my then boyfriend and I were given his parents' orchestra tickets for an evening performance of *Tosca*. It was the first time I had had a real seat at an opera, but, in truth, sitting with such an extremely well-behaved audience, some of whom even dared to fall asleep, made the experience feel overly refined and lifeless.

In my senior year, I began to skip school—a lot. My friend Diana and I had started hanging out in the West

Village. She played double bass and had older brothers who knew about jazz musicians like Miles Davis, Charlie Mingus, Thelonious Monk, Horace Silver and the trio Lambert Henricks & Ross. We traveled into the city to hear performances whenever we could. I am still not sure how we were able to get into those clubs because we were clearly underage. But we always went to early evening sets and sometimes to afternoon performances at places like the Blue Note, the Village Gate, and the Village Vanguard, so we were able to see many of these incredible musicians perform live. We were at Carnegie Hall for the famous concert when Nina Simone refused to stop playing at the designated time, even after the unionized stage crew threatened to walk out, shut off the lights, and abandon her. She was our hero then, a true artist immersed in her craft, and we cheered her defiance.

My parents did not seem to care that we were hanging out in the Village during the days, which clearly meant we were playing hooky from school. My mother was always willing to write a note saying I was sick, which, in those days, I actually often was, although I am not sure why. Maybe I just needed time to myself. When Diana and I were not together, I also stayed home from school to read books like Ernest Jones's biography of Sigmund Freud and the work of other thinkers. Whenever a new James Baldwin novel or book of essays came out, I would write its name on a piece of paper and ask my mother to pick it up for me on her way home from work. Evanthes was on Forty-

Second Street and Broadway, and I knew she passed several bookstores en route to the subway. In this way, I acquired Baldwin's *Nobody Knows My Name, Another Country, The Fire Next Time*, and then found his older works, such as *Go Tell it on the Mountain* and *Giovanni's Room*. I realize now I was living a very isolated, internal life: reading the *New York Times Book Review*, evaluating what I wanted to learn, and getting those books when I could. It was the beginning of my intellectual development, something my parents could not share. Still, they never discouraged it.

In 1964 or '65, maybe at one of the Village clubs that we frequented, I met a handsome young man who told me he worked at the World's Fair as a "Watusi dancer." He said that many Black dancers from the Bronx and Harlem were performing at the fair, pretending to be Africans. I must have given him my phone number because he called one day. I had my own telephone extension in my room then but I did not have my own number. By chance, my father, who was downstairs, also picked up the call. When I hung up, George came into my room, livid. "This man you were talking to is Black. What are you doing giving your number to men like that? Why do you think these men are interested in a girl like you?" and so on. Nothing I could say calmed him. I am sure this event led to another fight or a period in which we were not talking to each other. But in those days, I was moving in the world of Black culture all the time—in music, in literature, and in the Village. Having grown up in Crown Heights, this world did not seem foreign or odd to me. I could not understand, nor did I want to understand, why my father was acting out this underlying need to control me, which was dominating his behavior.

George was racist. He often talked about the "changes" happening in New York. His remarks had to do with his perception that Blacks were "taking over" the city. My mother remained silent at such times; she was not really complicitous, but she did not stand up to him about these statements either, at least not in front of me. Although I had heard this kind of talk before, it nonetheless surprised me, especially because my parents were not conventional or small-minded around many other issues. They did not have much investment in the status quo. They had married across religions, which among Jews and Catholics in the 1930s and 1940s was almost equivalent to marrying across racial lines. Their close friends had never been traditionally middle class, politically conservative, or overtly racist. Nor were they provincial; they were New Yorkers. Otherness was interesting to them, especially to my mother who knew many "show people." Some were Gay. Some were Brown. Some were Black. By the 1960s the staff at Evanthes was also quite diverse. Yet my father was remarkably, overtly, unselfconsciously, unapologetically racist, as were many of the people with whom he did business.

DETOUR TO THE MAFIA

After my mother returned to working at Evanthes, she often spoke very fondly about a young man who "came up to her place" for scalp treatments. His name was Frank and he had been a junior high school math teacher until he became a horse trainer. My mother was certain that his Italian family in Bensonhurst had "deep ties to the Mafia." When she first met him, he was already training horses for Hollywood celebrities, boarding their thoroughbreds at Belmont Racetrack in New York and at Santa Anita in Los Angeles. My mother and Marie had been placing bets with "Frankie" for years. And, as they said, "He always gave them good tips," which meant he never let them lose.

Although Frank was only in his twenties, my mother said his hair was already thinning and his hairline receding. He came to Evanthes, hoping they could help. I am sure my mother must have talked to him about me a great deal because he said he wanted to meet me. But we did not meet until I was in college. By that time, I was living in a world of "counterculture" and was not at all interested in meeting a straight-ahead neighborhood guy from Bensonhurst, who I feared might be racist and sexist like some other young men I had met from the Boroughs. I was sure we would never agree about issues like the Vietnam War. But my mother insisted I meet him and, finally, I consented.

So, one day when I was home for the summer, Frank came to the house—a tall, lean, sweet, cute guy who still had some black hair on his head (more than I had imagined from my mother's description). And, as I predicted, he could not have been more unlike my college friends. He wore white pants, a pale-blue button-down shirt, white patent leather shoes with shiny buckles, no socks, a few bangles, multiple gold chains, and, on one of these, a large black enameled cross studded with rhinestones. He drove an enormous white Cadillac with white leather interior and gold trim, which he parked in front of our house.

Although he was not much older than I was, it was clear that he was already making a lot of money. He told me he had started classes at a community college but could not focus enough to finish. He had wanted to get a master's degree in education and was impressed that I had plans to go to graduate school and get a PhD in literature. For now, he said, he was into the horse business, and he insisted on taking me to the track. I was returning to college in two days and had much to do to get ready, but I promised I would go with him to Belmont the next time I was in the city. On that first visit, we only had time for a walk around the neighborhood. He bought me a spumoni ice cream and we talked about our lives. On my next trip home, my mother had arranged for him to take me to Belmont. I was happy enough to see him again and was definitely interested in getting to know the "backside of the track"— a unique experience that only Frank could offer.

He picked me up in a new, equally enormous white Cadillac, and we were off. Once at Belmont, I could see that he was extremely natural, calm, and loving with the horses—and they seemed quite relaxed with him. I wondered how a boy from Brooklyn, who surely had not had a horse as a child, had learned so much about these magnificent creatures and was so comfortable with them. I also could see why my mother liked him. He had the best qualities of the Boroughs—respect for his elders, love of family, and a kind of charming chivalry that was lacking in my encounters with young men in college.

On the way home, he asked if I wanted to drive the car. I said, "Why not?" I knew I might never have another chance to drive a Cadillac. But very soon into our trip back to the city, a red light started flashing on the dashboard. Frank thought I was some kind of prodigy when I said that it was the oil light. I asked, "Is there oil in the car? When was the last time it was changed?" He had no idea. I told him that we should not drive the car while that light was flashing or we could blow the engine. He was impressed again that I knew such things. But anyone who ever took driver's education to get a license at sixteen, like I did, desperate to drive myself out of Brooklyn, would have known that.

I started to pull the car over, but Frank asked if we could drive just a bit farther to the diner he saw up ahead, which was announcing itself with a strobing red arrow pointing to an "Eat Here" sign. There, in pre-cell phone days, we at least would be able to telephone and get some help. When I called my parents from the diner to say I would be late, they did not seem concerned. "Oh, you are with Frankie," my mother said, "we won't worry." When I called two hours later to tell them we were still at the diner waiting for the tow truck, I woke up my mother. Because it was getting very late and there was still no sign of the truck, I called to say we were eating French fries at the diner and waiting for a taxi to take us to the city. "It's okay," my mother said. "You're in good hands." I asked her if my father was worried. "No, not at all," she said. "Why would he be?"

It was 5 a.m. when we finally made it back to Brooklyn. No one was waiting up, anxious that I was out with a Mafioso-kind of guy in the middle of the night, somewhere on a highway on Long Island in a broken-down car. Frank was familiar to my parents and therefore safe—white, Italian, and from Brooklyn. He was a horse trainer, an occupation they could understand—marginal, like some of their friends and my parents themselves. He might as well have been family.

I went back to college and did not see Frank again for several years, not until I was a graduate student at the University of California, San Diego and I was living on the beach in Del Mar, very close to the racetrack. In those days, I often went to the track with a dear friend, Joe Sommers, a working-class guy from Queens, who was chair of the literature department at the university and who also loved the horses.

When I saw the racing form for the week, I noticed that

Frank had horses running. I thought he might actually be in Del Mar, where lots of the trainers stayed, so I left a note for him at the clubhouse. I was not really expecting that he would respond or even get the message, but he called the next day. I then went to see him and his team— they were all living together in a big townhouse in Cardiff-by-the-Sea, quite near my bungalow in Del Mar. Much about Frank had changed. He was still training horses for some very big Hollywood stars and others, but now he had an empire. His employees seemed to adore him, and I realized that he was quite a smart and charismatic guy. But something about him was different. He was moving erratically, talking fast, jumping from one topic to the next, unable to sit still. Also, that sweetness I had seen in Brooklyn was less apparent. Although he was still kind and generous with me, and with those who worked for him, he was somehow more agitated while running on a kind of wild energy. He took me around, introducing me to more of his employees, telling them about me and me about them. He didn't seem to want to be in any situation where we would be alone and actually able to talk. A month later, Frank sent a car to bring me to visit him in L.A. where he was running horses at Santa Anita. During that trip I began to suspect that he was on drugs. Only later, when I saw that same kind of manic, aggrandized behavior up close again in a boyfriend of mine, did I understand that the Frank I had observed in Del Mar and in L.A. was on serious amounts of cocaine.

Some years later, I asked my mother if she had heard anything about him. "Oh Frankie," she said, brushing off the question, as if she barely knew him and cared even less. "He was deep into debt to the Mafia, you know. Who can tell what became of him? Could be at the bottom of the East River for all I know." "Mom," I said, shocked at how cold and disinterested she seemed. "Well, honey, you know, it's possible. He had some pretty tough friends."

In 1983, when I was living in Chicago, I saw a film about the Romani people entitled *Angelo My Love*, produced and directed by Robert Duvall. There on the screen, in a walk-on part, nearly playing himself, was an Italian guy, in a short, white, terry-cloth bathrobe, just out of the shower. He had lots of tousled black hair (must have been a wig) and several gold chains—definitely Frank. Luckily, his story had not ended as my mother had imagined.

BUFFALO

For my entire life, I had been dreaming of going to college. Education provided the guarantee that there would be a world beyond Brooklyn, that there would be travel and knowledge and languages and adventure. I had friends and cousins who never went to college, some who barely ever left Crown Heights. When they grew up, they chose to stay close to their parents in Brooklyn or moved to Queens with their children. Few barely ever ventured into Manhattan. I had other plans.

My father of course did not want me to go away to school. He absolutely did everything he could to convince me to stay in the city and attend Brooklyn College. In those days I loved cars, so he even offered to buy me a used MG Midget. Although Brooklyn College was, and still is, a first-rate school where amazing people have taught and been taught, it is literally right across the street from Midwood High School, where I had just spent the previous three years.

I had little knowledge about where I should go to college, and no one to consult about it. So, when one of my Midwood schoolmates, with whom I studied French and Latin, said she was applying to the State University of New York at Buffalo, I did the same. I knew we could afford a state school. I planned to study English and American literature and as it turned out, the school's English department was ideal for me. It had been founded by poet Charles Olsen at a time when then Governor Nelson Rockefeller had poured a great deal of money into the university. Olson was able to assemble an extraordinary faculty, who had followed him from Black Mountain College, an experimental, interdisciplinary, non-degree program in Asheville, North Carolina, where artist and writer teachers also ran the school. As a result, the English department at Buffalo was radical and creatively oriented, home to writers John Barth, Gregory Corso, Robert Creeley, Ed Dorn, and Leslie Fiedler. Allen Ginsburg and Peter Orlovsky were often on campus, as were Denise Levertov and Diane di Prima.

Although the program was extremely intellectual, the atmosphere was more like an art school.

Surprisingly, when it came time for me to leave for college, my father insisted on driving me to Buffalo, quite a gesture for someone who avoided driving whenever he could. Perhaps he thought that this might be our last road trip together and hoped there would be time for us to talk. Although I cannot remember anything meaningful about the trip itself, I do remember that when he said goodbye, before heading back to Brooklyn, he was crying. I did not actually understand his tears at the time. But I do now. Perhaps as karmic punishment for having been so oblivious to my father's deep pain at losing me to college, I have had to relive this moment repeatedly at various dormitories in Chicago and New York, as I watched generations of students being dropped off by their parents at the beginning of each school year. The students always seem ecstatic to be almost on their own—the moment of independence very near—but the parents, oh the parents, they are most often completely bereft. They know that their own lives are about to change radically, as they lose their children to the future. I was sad to say goodbye to my father in the parking lot near my dorm but, in my thinking, I would be home for Thanksgiving, which was not far off. Yet, of course, it was not the same as being dropped off at the bus station for summer camp, knowing I would be returning to live at home with my parents once summer ended. This time was different. It was the beginning of my life without them and theirs without me.

I am sure my father had many imaginings of the wildness of college and the boys, sex, drugs, and alcohol, that came with it. These fears, combined with his understanding of the anarchic nature of collective adolescent behavior, were more than well founded. He truly was about to lose control of me. But other parents were about to lose much more.

THE LOST GIRL

On that first day at college, right after I left George, I unexpectedly encountered my father's worst nightmare about my potential future, embodied in the person of my freshman roommate, Evelyn.

When I walked into what was to be our shared room, Evelyn was leaning sideways over an ironing board that was raised as high as it could go. Her long, obviously dyed, very black hair, was draped across it like a piece of stiff cloth. I noted that the iron was set on "synthetic," and she was moving it across her hair with rhythmic strokes. I had only observed someone doing this once before, at summer camp. Because the board was not tall enough for her to iron comfortably, Evelyn's position looked strained. Whenever I see the 1943 Balthus painting *Patience*—a young girl leaning sideways over a small desk in a most awkward posture—I remember that first sighting of Evelyn.

Many of my Jewish girlfriends with a certain type of hair worried about frizzing, especially in the rain, and tried everything to straighten it. Even a half-Jewish girl like me suffered this anxiety. I slept on large, empty frozen-orange-juice cans for many years in an attempt to forestall my hair's unruliness. If I turned on my side while sleeping, the edges of the cans pressed deeply into my scalp. When it was wet outside, I wore two or three plastic rain hats while walking to school. But as soon as I took them off, the barometric pressure always won out: first there were waves, then there were curls, then there was frizz.

In those days, universities had no real system for pairing roommates, no attempt to prepare each for the other beforehand. There was no Facebook, IM chatrooms, FaceTime, Instagram, Google surveys, or Zoom. The student affairs administrators in charge of roommate assignments made certain assumptions. Those at SUNY-Buffalo probably thought, rightly, that because Evelyn and I were both Jewish (at least by our names), both from the Boroughs—Queens and Brooklyn, which, at that time, meant we were probably either "working class" or lower middle class—that we would be compatible roommates. But what logic—ethnic, geographic, or socioeconomic— could ever have prepared me for Evelyn?

Our roles were established from the start: she was the awkward, inexperienced girl from Queens, and I the more-savvy one from Brooklyn. On our first evening together, she asked me how to wash socks. "You're kidding?" I said, "have you really never washed your own socks?" "No, never," she said. Her helplessness and lack of worldliness at all levels was both annoying and endearing. Evelyn did not try to hide what she did not know or pretend to be sophisticated in ways she was not. She often recognized the absurdity of situations, even the act of ironing her hair and laughed easily and readily at herself. She also had a sweetness about her and enthusiasm for the unique qualities of others. I liked her immediately. Perhaps more important, I trusted her and also felt that she had been entrusted to me, but I had no idea why. Although Evelyn was not a wild girl when we met, I soon understood that she was already a lost girl.

The more she told me about her life, the more I realized how sheltered and lonely she had been. Her father was a high school science teacher; her brother was older and had immigrated to Australia where, as a researcher, he experimented with LSD. Her brother was quite absent from her life but had never related to her much anyway. She loved her father and saw the goodness in him, but he too was mostly silent. She hardly spoke about her mother. They all lived in a small bungalow in Queens, each searching, it seemed, for psychic space. Her father found it in the basement, where he built miniature ships in bottles. Evelyn retreated into fashion magazines. Obsessed as she was with clothes and makeup, daily life was only a preparation for the romance she was yet to experience. Her desires were adolescent, but she was aware of that and unapologetic for it.

Evelyn was striking, with all that black hair and thick,

black eyeliner and coal, dark eye shadow, Goth before her time, but she was not really pretty. She had had her nose done, like other Jewish girls I knew. In those days, everyone who underwent this surgery received similar noses, easily recognized as having been "fixed." Surely each girl felt that her new nose was a vast improvement over the one she had been given at birth. I was not so sure. When I visited one of my summer-camp friends soon after she had had that operation, I was shocked. Large black-and-blue blotches circled her eyes. There was also a great deal of swelling, and, of course, lots of bandaging and cotton stuffing inside her nose. She looked as if she had been hit by a car. I could only imagine how painful that all must have been. But my friend had been determined to "get a nose job." I'm sure Evelyn had been as well. These young women just could not accept what they saw as a massive imperfection. If you spent enough time reading those teen magazines, you would have found fault with everything about yourself. At that time, the images of the perfect teenage girl—very white, with tall, thin, long, straight, very blond hair—had nothing to do with the features of Jewish girls or the actual bodies of anyone else I knew.

In our cinder-block dorm room, Evelyn and I slept on two small wooden single beds, low to the floor, like bunk beds that were not stacked. We shared a bathroom with our "suite mates," both of whom were from upstate New York. They too seemed matched by religion, region, and class. We were the girls from "the Boroughs," they from the

"Sticks." They imagined that we probably had already seen it all, maybe even had done it all. They clustered together in the early months, as did those of us from "the city." The clothes, humor, and small-town-ness of the upstate girls reminded me of those of my Polish relatives who had never left Pennsylvania. From time to time, the resident assistants, or RAs, tried to bring the two groups together. They held floor meetings to encourage us to talk about our histories, hoping to break down the barriers, but it never really worked. We city girls were arrogant. We assumed that the upstate girls would go back to their hometowns and become grade-school or gym teachers. We imagined their aspirations, not related to their intelligence, were set on lesser goals than ours. College was tough for all of us, and we grew to like and respect each other just for getting through the classes, happy when any of us did well. But we were never really close—they were too shy, and we were terrible snobs.

Most of the girls on our floor worked hard. Evelyn was the anomaly. From the first, she did not even try to study, although she had done so in high school or would never have been admitted to the university. Instead, she literally spent hours at the mirror experimenting with different types of makeup and hairstyles. The rest of us knew her behavior was odd and inappropriate given what we had come to college to achieve, yet we did not know what to do about it or how to explain it. Evelyn was like the madwoman in the attic or the deranged sister we had to hide from the world. I used to imagine that when she became old, Evelyn would be like Crazy Mary, the woman who lived near my grandmother's farm in Pennsylvania and walked the country roads in ripped, baggy, dirty clothes wearing a metal bowl on her head like a hat. Something terrible must have happened to Mary, but no one seemed to know what. The local farmers' wives left food and clothing on her doorstep. We children left our used comic books, the only things we owned that we thought she might like. I already saw a future time when Evelyn might be lost to us in just such ways.

Evelyn was physically awkward. Her feet splayed out when she walked, which made her a bit comical; she exaggerated moving in this way when she wanted to make us laugh. Not sure-footed, she was excessively fearful of falling, slipping, and sliding, especially on ice. When we crossed streets together, she always hung onto one of us. Large intersections and fast cars frightened her. I joined the ski club in the second semester of our freshman year, and Evelyn said she wanted to come with me. So, we rode together on the bus for an evening of night skiing. In Buffalo, the hills were icy and treacherous, and the sun never seemed to shine in winter. Skiing at night was not that different than skiing during the day. That evening, not only did Evelyn refuse to even try to put on skis, she would not even walk out of the lodge, fearful of falling on ice. She sat at the bar the whole evening, drinking hot chocolate and talking to the bartender. She showed much self-derision about her fears, phobias, compulsions, and bad habits, but she gave no indication that she could ever overcome or unlearn them.

Evelyn never ate a real meal that first year in the dormitory. She survived on French fries and binged on candy bars. She hardly went out during the day and, when she ventured forth at night, she often dressed monochromatically: tight, royal-blue wool pants and a matching royal-blue sweater, or orange—all orange. She wore a short, cream-colored, fake-fur jacket with a hood and sprayed herself with perfume each time she left the dorm. It was as if we were at a resort and all she had to do was spend her days dressing for dinner. College for her was only about boys, fraternity parties, and the exultant freedom of being away from her family. I have seen something of this behavior in other freshmen students since, but most eventually settle into the meaning of why they are there and do the work. Evelyn never did.

I understood her desire to be free of the pressure she and I both had lived with throughout high school. She also had studied a great deal, especially math and science, just to get into college. But now, she seemed uninterested in all of it. I did not judge her partying and drinking; I was doing the same. But unlike her, I was propelled both by a fear of returning to Brooklyn having failed and also by my powerful desire to become educated. She was oblivious to both.

Evelyn also did not sleep, at least not when the rest of

us did. She was awake most of the night, wandering the halls in her nightgown and light-blue pom-pom slippers, looking for someone to talk to. Because she did not even try to sleep at night, she never made it to her morning classes. In the beginning, I attempted to wake her before I left for my 8 a.m. German class each day, but when I would come back at 10 a.m., she still would be asleep. Eventually, I stopped trying. She was happiest when we were all awake, "pulling an all-nighter," usually on Dexedrine, to write our papers or to study for a biology exam.

She admired those of us working to get through classes and was impressed with our determination, focus, care, and interest. But Evelyn did not share any of it. There was a tenuousness about her, as if the rest of us were unduly tethered to the world and its obligations, conventions, expectations, but she was not. This positioning of herself was not self-conscious. It was neither the rebelliousness of artists who deliberately upend convention nor that of political radicals who stand tangential to society in order to critique it. Although at times she did seem joyful, Evelyn's lightness of being was far from enviable. Hers was not an evolved sense of personal freedom. Rather, her demeanor signaled an obliviousness that made us worry that she could simply slip away. Although we were aware of Evelyn's psychological and physical precarity, we had not fully recognized that her behavior could later manifest in even more destructive ways. We, who had not yet lost the world, were unable to imagine the consequences of things.

It was 1965 and we were listening to Bob Dylan nonstop. My friend Diana and I had first seen him in Forest Hills performing with Joan Baez, barefoot on the stage and still unknown to most of the audience. He had already written "Blowin' in the Wind" made famous by the folk group Peter, Paul and Mary. But now he was singing his own songs to huge audiences who were seeing him perform for the first time. Dylan was about to go electric and to become, and stay, big. *"It's a hard rain's a-gonna fall."* His words filled our nights and our days.

THE BREAKS

Evelyn's parents called her every week, and they sent packages of food, money, even clothes. She was sweet with them on the phone, but she never told them anything about her life. When it came time for Christmas break, she surprised me by asking if she could come home with me. My parents agreed, so she and I took a long car ride with other students from Buffalo to Brooklyn. I was on a tight, three-week, study schedule. Exams, punishingly, came after the holidays, so during the break I had to read thirty plays for a class in world drama and write several papers about nineteenth-century novels for another.

During that visit, Evelyn knew she had to let me study, for at least some hours a day, but nonetheless she never left the house. She would not have ventured forth into an unknown neighborhood alone or gone to a restaurant or museum on her own, especially in the snow. We stayed together on the top floor of my parent's house, seeing them mostly for dinners. Each day, Evelyn would wait until I was free to "play," and then we talked or listened to music. I am sure my parents thought she was odd, but they never mentioned anything to me. While she was with us, she wore no makeup or tight clothing. She pulled her hair back into a ponytail, barely changed out of her pajamas, and was kind and shy.

My Polish mother was a great cook, including of Italian food, so there was an enormous selection of things to eat: lasagna, manicotti, braciole, and, for dessert, homemade Polish krushchiki and Chocolate Blackout Cake from Ebbinger's. The food was endless and, surprisingly to me, so was Evelyn's appetite. But after dinner most nights, she would go upstairs and vomit it all up—a behavior I had never seen before. I did not understand this pattern then, but of course I realize now that Evelyn had become bulimic, or always had been and had hidden it well from the rest of us. It was obvious to me that this behavior was unhealthy, but I did not yet understand where such a disorder might come from or where it could lead.

After Christmas, we returned to school, and Evelyn's life continued in the same way. She still did not attend classes; she slept all day and partied at night. One evening she came back to the dorm so drunk that she had to be carried to her room. This behavior generated a warning from the RA: "If this happens again, you will be OUT of the dorm." Because freshmen were required to live in the dormitory, being kicked out of the dorm meant that Evelyn would have to leave school. But she continued sneaking in late at night and soon developed a "rep" for being too easy with boys.

Then came the fire drill. Whether it was a real fire, a thought-to-be-real fire, or just a drill, we never knew. But at 3 a.m. one morning, the RAs came running through the corridors yelling, "Wake up. Get out of your rooms NOW." We were all asleep, except for Evelyn. She probably had never gone to bed, but she refused to leave the dorm. She told me, firmly, "I will not go out without my makeup. I'd rather burn." At first, I thought she was kidding, but she was not. I tried every argument to get her to move, but she was convinced the fire was not real. "Why all the fuss? It's just a drill. Why should we go?" We were the last ones left on the floor. The RA came in twice, threatening to call the campus police. "Out now," she said. I grabbed Evelyn's fake-fur coat from the chair, threw it over her shoulders, and literally dragged her from the room. She was furious with me. Now, I thought, they will surely throw her out of the dormitory, but this was only strike two.

Buffalo was a dreary place all winter, every winter, overhung with dark skies and with "more snow than Alaska," as the locals liked to say. Soon after Thanksgiving, parked cars would be buried in a white crypt and not seen again until the spring thaw. Our dorm room was overheated by radiators we could not control, so we kept the windows cracked open, and the air filled with the smell of snow—damp and a bit metallic. To get away from the Buffalo bleakness and to have some fun, Evelyn and I decided to go to Miami for spring break, unbeknownst to our families. I cannot recall how we came to this decision—maybe because others in the university were doing so or because we had read about student parties at Fort Lauderdale. As hard as it is for me to imagine now, all that madness sounded great to me then.

At that time, if you were twenty-one or younger, you could fly at half-price. We could afford the tickets and so we went. We arrived in Miami at night with no hotel reservations and little money. None of this made us the least anxious. On the contrary—we were excited.

We got a cab at the airport and asked the driver to take us to a cheap hotel. He drove us to a typical three-story Florida motel, with a gangway outside each floor, in what was then the Black part of Miami, probably close to downtown. He spoke to the manager, who helped us carry our bags up the outside stairs and showed us a room on the second floor with two large beds. The driver was a very nice guy and said he would come by the next morning to see how we were doing. We had no geographic sense of where we were, but we could tell we were not near the beach. The motel seemed a bit rowdy—there were parties going on in other rooms that were spilling into the parking lot, and there were doors opening and closing all night. Exhausted, and now a bit unnerved by the grunginess of the place, we pushed the dresser in front of the door—a precaution I have since repeated whenever I have felt unsafe in an unknown location—and went to sleep.

In the morning we heard a rap on the window. It was the driver. He said he wanted to introduce us to someone. Standing next to him on the gangway was a small, muscular, Black man in a sleeveless tee and a doo rag. That's how we first met Hank Ballard and, later, the members of his band, the Midnighters. Hank seemed surprised to find two young white girls staying in this motel, but he was very friendly and invited us to come out with them that night to a club where they were performing.

I surely knew who Hank Ballard was. He had written "Finger Poppin' Time," which had been big on the pop charts and had even been nominated for a Grammy Award. However, I did not know, but soon would learn, that he also had written and been the first to record "The Twist," which did not become a hit until Chubby Checker recorded it soon afterward. The song then went really big, but not for Hank. He was bitter that he had missed making a fortune and felt frustrated that he was still playing the third-rate-club circuit.

That night, as promised, the cab driver returned to take us to the nightclub. We got dressed up as best we could and headed for another unknown part of Miami. Evelyn and I were the only White people at the club: two young

Jewish girls, probably too young for the scene, but no one said a word—we were with the band. Everyone made us feel welcome. Hank Ballard and the Midnighters put on an incredible performance of music and dance, but the show was not just them, it was also everyone on the dance floor.

I loved to dance and still do. In those days we used to do the Twist, Watusi, Monkey, Boston Monkey, Swim, Hitchhike, Walk the Dog, Pony, Chicken, Funky Chicken, and Frug. I won a Mashed Potatoes contest while dancing with Skippy Blumberg at a Friday night "mixer" in Buffalo and, years later, won a Twist contest in Chicago dancing with a younger friend. But I have never again seen anything like this dance floor in Miami. Large, fabulously dressed women in glittery tops came out of the audience with their partners. The women then hiked up their skirts, very high, and got way down low and up against the guys, back and front. The dancing was raw and powerful. Everything I had seen on dance floors until then seemed juvenile in comparison.

The next day Hank offered us his pink Cadillac to go to the beach. I could not say no. I drove. Evelyn never could or would drive. While parking the big, ostentatious, pink-flamingo car at South Beach, we saw a group of guys we knew from Buffalo, who were also there for Spring Break. Of course, they asked about the car. I told them that we had met Hank Ballard and that this was his car. When we returned to college, the story was everywhere—we were hanging out with Black men in Miami, we "liked" Black men, and, in the racist parlance of the day, we were "n—lovers."

We did not stay at that hotel for the entire week because we really wanted to be near the beach. But on a last restless night before we moved on, we went walking. There wasn't much around, just highways and cars. Soon a patrol car pulled up and the police started interrogating us: "Why are you here in this neighborhood? What are you doing out so late? Do you have ID's?" At first, I did not realize that they thought we were sex workers. Two young White girls in a rundown Black area appeared incongruous to them—and of course it was, but not in the way they thought.

We didn't have our purses with us because it seemed safer to go out without them. The police drove us back to the motel to check our ID's, and the manager was not happy to see us pull up in a police car. When the police learned that we were college students on spring break, they took us to the station and insisted on calling our parents to ask if they knew we were there. It was late, and they woke up my father, asking him if he knew I was in Miami. "No, he said, he "did not." Then my father asked to speak to me. I was terrified of how he would respond, but all he said was, "Get the hell out of the South. Those guys are anti-Semitic." The police never called Evelyn's parents, to her great relief.

My father didn't mention that call again until some months later when I was back in New York for the summer, working in the Village selling expensive Mexican dresses at Fred Leighton's off Eighth Street, living at home with my parents. One day, my light-blue (to match my room) Princess "extension" phone rang. I was upstairs and my father was downstairs. Again, we both picked up the phone at the same moment. This time it was Hank Ballard—Hank's voice: smoky, mature, smooth, and deep. He said, "Hey, baby...." I cannot remember more than that. He probably had wanted to see me, but although I had enjoyed meeting him in Miami, I had not planned on meeting up with him again.

I quickly got off the phone because I could imagine the accusations that were likely to follow, and soon my father was in my room. "Who is this guy? Why is he calling? What do you think a guy like that wants from you?" I told him that Evelyn and I had met Hank and the Midnighters in Florida. I explained their records and successes and how gracious Hank had been to us, but exactly how could I explain the actual innocence of it all? Soon we were in another fight—a truly nasty one, about race, men, his fears, and my refusal to back down. "What is wrong," I insisted, "with meeting a smart, talented, and kind person?" Our positions were irreconcilable. We just could not talk about anything related to men, and Black men in particular, without my father assuming that something sleazy either happened, would happen, or could happen.

By spring semester, Evelyn, who continued to sleep through her classes, was on probation, and she was pregnant. At least the boy offered to pay half the cost of the abortion and drove her to Wisconsin where it was then legal to get one. Needless to say, he soon after disappeared. But Evelyn was haunted by what she had done. She told me that she kept seeing the fetus struggling, and the pain of this image drove her into a deep sadness. She was never one to be unhappy and yet now she was suffering guilt, both for having gotten pregnant and for having had an abortion. Soon she became silent, even with me.

I went home for the summer and worked in a bookstore on Eighth Street in the Village. Evelyn, having been told that she could not return to the university in the fall, went to live in the city and find a "real" job. Her college life was officially over.

THE GREAT NORTHERN HOTEL

In her 2016 biography of the sculptor Isamu Noguchi, Hayden Herrera writes about a time when Noguchi returns to New York City from Japan, completely broke. He ends up living at the Great Northern Hotel–a place he returned to again and again at various other periods in his life. I was surprised to read a reference to this hotel, which I had visited often because Evelyn lived there right after she left college and then again at other times in subsequent years. The Great Northern Hotel used to be next to Carnegie Hall at 118 East Fifty-Seventh Street. It was shabby but safe, and the location was ideal. The musty lobby was filled with overstuffed, dark-green, velour couches and brown leather armchairs. It was mostly a residential hotel, like the Algonquin and many other New York hotels at that time.

Although Evelyn was living a very different life than the rest of us—and was no longer physically nearby—our small group of college classmates remained close to her and made sure to see her when we came into the city from Buffalo. During my visits, I would sit on the edge of the bed (there was only a bed and a "vanity" with a very large mirror), and we would talk while she put on her makeup. But it became increasingly difficult to pretend that the life Evelyn was living now made sense to any of us. She had met someone named Guy, who was probably twenty years older than she was. She was convinced he loved her, and he might have. But while living at the Great Northern Hotel, Evelyn had become a sex worker. Guy, we learned, set her up with various "johns." She insisted he was not a pimp, just her boyfriend—this work was simply how they supported themselves.

At the hotel she had the same routine that she had had in college—staying up all night, sleeping all day. A great deal of her time was spent getting ready to go out. She would call the men in her book to arrange a time and place to meet. They never came to her hotel and they did not know where she lived, how to reach her, or her real name. She was known to them as Corrinne Cohn. She played the college girl with these men—someone trying to get money to go back to school. For the most part, she did not seem unhappy with this life. The only anxiety she ever expressed to me took the form of a recurring, imagined scenario: she would set up a meeting with a man in her "john book," who was listed with a pseudonym, of course, and that person would turn out to be her father or a friend of her family's—someone who would recognize her and tell her parents what she was doing.

In our sophomore year, a group of us rented the nastiest apartment I have ever lived in. It was on the ground floor in the back of a small, decrepit building. It was so dreary and rundown that when my parents came to visit, my father refused to go inside, and my mother, who did go in, began to cry. But having escaped the dormitory, this space represented freedom. When Evelyn came to visit, she stayed there with us. We always picked her up at the airport because we knew she was afraid to take a taxi or a bus alone. During the day, while we were in school or working at odd jobs, she would wait at our apartment for us to return from class, just as she always had done. We were "girlfriends" to her, like those she had had in high school, only better, because we did not compete with her or want to become her.

One typically freezing, sleeting, miserable, dark day in Buffalo, we got a frantic call from Guy to say that Evelyn would be arriving by plane at 2 p.m. that afternoon. "Could you pick her up? She had to leave New York," he said. Our friend Emily and I went to meet Evelyn at the airport, uncertain why there was so much drama around this visit.

At that time, you could wait at the arrival gates, so there we were when the plane landed. But even after everyone had exited the plane, we could not find Evelyn. I thought we must not have seen her or that she had missed the plane. Soon, a woman in a big, blond, Afro wig, wearing dark sunglasses, a bulky fake-leopard-skin coat, velvet bell-bottoms, and white go-go boots, came up to me. "It's Evelyn," she whispered, giggling. "It's me." "But why are you dressed like that?" I asked her. "I'll tell you in the car."

As it turns out, Guy had bought her a new "john book." They had paid ten thousand dollars for it (an astronomical amount to us). But, unbeknownst to Evelyn or Guy, the men in the book were into S&M. It took Evelyn two dates to figure this out. After the second incident, she and Guy told the sellers of the book that they wanted their money back. But these men were Mafiosi and not about to refund the money or make an exchange. These sellers had threatened them both, so Guy had sent Evelyn to us. He called a hundred times a day to see if she was okay. There were no cell phones then, so these calls came directly into the house and drove us mad. He worried for her safety—and his own. We worried for her sanity—and our own. We asked her how and why she was continuing this lifestyle with him. She thought we were exaggerating the dangers and believed, as if she were in a movie, that there would be a happy resolution and that soon she and Guy would have saved enough money that she would not have to work again. But, of course, we did not trust Guy and we surely did not trust where this life might take her.

I was carrying a heavy course load in English and American literature during this time and still getting up early for German classes. When I wasn't studying, I was working—at first operating a Bruning copy machine, a big, clunky thing that constantly needed ink, the precursor to the Xerox photocopier. I was also working as a waitress at Bill's Delicatessen, trying to steer people away from the tuna fish, which always sat in the cooler for far too long. I was endlessly busy and always tired. I had little time or patience for Evelyn's drama, but, mostly, I was scared for her.

Soon after the Mafia incident, Evelyn vowed to get a straight job. And she did, as a receptionist in a travel agency. She, who had never traveled anywhere and only knew Queens and Buffalo and barely those, was completely unprepared to help anyone plan a vacation. But Evelyn was smart, and she could be charming on the phone. That first week, wearing high heels, she slid on the office's polished floor and broke her leg. Then, truly helpless, she went back to Guy. She had no money. She had no skills. And, of course, Guy was waiting, only too happy for her to support him again, and to resume their life together as soon as her leg healed.

CALIFORNIA

After college, I moved to San Diego for graduate school. Evelyn and I were still in touch. We only saw each other when we were on the same coast, but I usually knew where she was living, although not much more. One summer, when we were both in San Francisco, we arranged to meet. I was having dinner with a group of underground comics artists whom Evelyn and I both knew from Buffalo—one of them was Spain, the inventor of *Trashman* and *Phlegm Man* who had once been the partner of our dear friend Karen. He was a kind person with a scary imagination, close to R. Crumb, Aline Kominsky-Crumb, and other counterculture comic book artists at that time.

Evelyn arrived at the restaurant late, heavily made up, wearing a black, velvet cape, under which she wore a white, see-through, antique-lace blouse that was completely open in the back, and no bra. She wore tight, black velvet, hip-huggers that exposed her navel. During that hippie era, when women's fashion was going in the opposite direction—natural, no makeup—Evelyn appeared ghost-like and artificial. I noticed people at other tables laughing at her.

Always a sweet spirit—loving and shy—she now was flaunting her sexuality and promiscuity. Her clothes were blatantly designed to seduce men, although it never really was men she wanted. It was love. Friendship. Except for Guy and our small college group, she had no other important relationships that I knew of. During this encounter, I could see that she was even more unbalanced than the last time I had seen her and had become almost a parody of herself and freakish to the world.

She and I were soon together again in San Diego, in the low-scrub Anza-Borrego desert, where I was living with my then boyfriend Michael. I was a graduate student at the University of California, San Diego. We were staying in an old migrant worker's shack that Michael had renovated as a rustic cottage, in a location that, at that time, was still undeveloped and remote. Evelyn was returning to New York from Hawaii. I can no longer remember for how long she visited, but I do remember how she looked then in flip-flops, standing in the kitchen wearing one of my Mexican dresses—off-white, coarse linen, empire waist, with embroidered blue flowers on the skirt. Her skin was very pale with no makeup, and her black hair was pulled into a ponytail. She seemed so delicate, so young, and, for a moment, I thought she could start over with a different life.

Evelyn was impressed that we lived in what to her was an extremely wild place and that I was not afraid to be there alone at times. She, of course, would never walk with me in the desert, but I told her about the creatures who shared our environment: rattlesnakes, scorpions, black widow spiders, tarantulas, pygmy skunks, coyotes, and a solitary bobcat. It amazed and terrified her that this is where we chose to live, but she liked being with us and was delighted that I had a boyfriend who appeared to care enough to bring me a glass of water in the middle of the night. These types of normal things, neither excessive nor unusual, were often extraordinary to her.

California was liberating. There I found the physical and even mental well-being that I had never experienced on the East Coast. I ate organic food. I ran up and down the hills on Black Mountain Road and swam in the ocean most days. I studied martial arts. I also took all kinds of psychedelic drugs, exploring my consciousness. My political friends and I engaged in radical politics, and so eventually our phones were tapped. I learned how to think seriously about the world. I fell in love, forgot about the unbearable weight of World War II and the Holocaust's darkness, and engaged in the collective battle against the war in Vietnam. We celebrated the liberation of Saigon, drinking Cuervo Gold tequila and dancing all night. I made friends for life and lost some as well. In the 1970s, many of us often traveled back and forth between California and New York. We traversed the country in "drive-away cars," delivering them to various destinations for a fee, or we flew for half-fare or for free anywhere as couriers for diplomatic correspondence. These opportunities do not exist anymore, but they were inexpensive ways to move around the world then, and we took advantage of them.

Evelyn and I, living truly different lives, nonetheless remained close. I don't know what brought her to us in San Diego or what was pulling her back to New York. She still had no purpose, no plan. She was floating in the ether, stopping to see those she loved along the way. A week or so later, Michael and I put her on a plane for New York. She and I were out of touch for some months, and when next I heard about her, she was dead.

I got a call. I don't remember from whom. There had been an accident. A man with whom Evelyn was involved, an addict as it turns out, had overdosed. Evelyn had been with him in the emergency room. She too had been shooting up but must have seemed okay because the nurses left her alone while they tried to resuscitate him. Evelyn waited to see if he would come through, but at some point, she went out. To buy cigarettes perhaps? Or sweets as those on heroin often do? While crossing the large, busy intersection, she lurched in front of a car and was hit. "She came out of nowhere," said the driver, who sat curbside, crying uncontrollably.

Fearful as she was, Evelyn would never have attempted to cross a large intersection alone—never, unless she was somehow out of body, perhaps drugged. We did not know she was using but concluded that she must have been very messed up at the time. They never should have let her out of the emergency room. Maybe she slipped or collapsed into the street. It was not the fault of the poor man who hit her, of this I was certain.

Evelyn was gone.

I wrote to her parents but I never heard back. None of us knew how to find her brother. Our friend Emily had gotten in touch with Alene, one of Evelyn's high school friends. Alene looked remarkably like Evelyn—dyed black hair, lots of makeup. She told Emily that Evelyn's mother had given her all of Evelyn's clothes. We thought that Alene now might also dress like Evelyn and pretend she had become her. Evelyn would have been furious about that.

A year later, while visiting my parents in Brooklyn, I was back on the third floor—where Evelyn and I had spent that dissolute Christmas together some years before, eating too much of my mother's lasagna. Suddenly, while sitting on my old, rickety attic bed, I felt Evelyn's spirit next to me. "I am bored," she said, "so bored." Bored now in death as she had been in life. Perhaps boredom always was the source of her problem. Nothing in her studies had ever engaged her enough, and what had engaged her was lethal. I was irritated by this intrusion into my psyche and by this reminder of the most troubling and least lovable part of herself. This visitation was not the first time Evelyn had appeared to me since her death—I had seen her image flitting by me several times—but this was the first time that she had spoken to me. Exacerbated, I responded, "You need to figure this out, Evelyn. You need to find your way in this other dimension. I don't know how to help you there." But my annoyance and rejection must have hurt her terribly. She had come to be with me and, unsympathetically, I had pushed her away. I so regret that I did not tell her then that I was sorry that she had died young, that I loved her and would never forget her.

Evelyn fell silent to me after that—there were no more appearances, no more wanting to be acknowledged or included—not until now, when, in the context of this book, I have felt compelled to tell her story, which is so intertwined with my own.

I wish I had not seen Evelyn's boredom as her failure or as my failure because I had not engaged her enough. But for boredom, I simply had no tolerance. I thought it was hers to find what in life could interest her, but she never did. In the past, whenever I encountered boredom in anyone, I would see it as a grave emptiness and would feel compelled, often fruitlessly and perhaps annoyingly to try to fill that empty space with activity or distraction. When my mother was in her late nineties and could no longer focus well enough to read, she would sit on the sofa looking out into the room. She seemed so bored to me that I tried many things to distract her. What I did not understand then is that she was not bored; she was reflecting on her life in those last years, absorbing it, giving it order. But because I equated boredom with death—hers and mine—I felt desperate to engage her in something, even when she clearly did not want to be taken out of the past and thrown into the present. I understood this only later when a dear friend was dying and was lucid enough to explain that, at this time, he simply wanted to be left alone to reexperience his life.

After the writer Sergei Esenin slashed his wrists in December 1925, Vladimir Mayakovsky wrote a requiem poem for him that contained these lines: "It is not difficult to die / To make life / Is more difficult by far." In April 1930, Mayakovsky also chose to take his own life.

Evelyn's trajectory was the very thing my father most feared for me. He was not wrong to think I could be vulnerable to destructive men, but he was wrong when he identified such men by their race. In those days, I was drawn to men who reminded me of him: confident, street-smart, handsome, but also elusive, which is how my father appeared to me when I was a child— often working late and gone from our everyday lives a good deal of the time. I indulged such men during my early adult years until I finally admitted to myself that I was psychically ill prepared to handle men who easily abandoned those they supposedly loved. Michael, my great love in California and Montana, was just such a man. I thought our life together would go on forever. But when he left me—or, rather, compromised our relationship so greatly that I was forced to leave him—I was shattered. His betrayal penetrated my spirit and threatened to rip it apart. Such men did divert me from my path for a time, but, propelled as I was by a deeper purpose and ambition, I survived and finally did learn to choose better, although my father did not believe that I ever would. Had he trusted me enough to have faith in my judgment, perhaps the cataclysm between us might never have occurred.

CHICAGO

As much as I had completely fallen in love with the ocean and the desert of southern California—and as engaged as I had been with the anti-war movement, the women's movement, and the United Farmworkers Union boycotts, by the late 1970s I knew it was time to head back East. I also felt I had spent too many years in academia and was eager to be out of that world for a time. Having completed my life's plan to receive a PhD in literature, I now needed to envision the rest of my life. So, I made an unexpected detour to Chicago to become part of the team starting a political newsweekly *In These Times*. In my mind, however, I was actually en route back home to New York, although, as it turned out, that return would take decades to accomplish.

Owner and publisher James Weinstein assembled progressive people from different parts of the country— writers, editors, and designers—to create an alternative publication. But by the time he and I met, the only still vacant position was that of office manager, something I had never done before and doubted I would be very good at. Still, it was an exciting adventure and worth a try. As I suspected, I was hardly adept at managing an office, but being part of this collective effort and helping to launch the project was fortuitous; it gave me an opportunity to write about art and popular culture in a journalistic context.

When I accepted the job, I had only a faint image of

what life in Chicago might be like, and it was formed by childhood excursions with my mother to visit her brothers who had migrated there after the mines closed in Pennsylvania. My uncle Lou, my aunt Marie, and my cousin Cindy lived "back of the yards," and my uncle Tony, aunt Emma, and their children lived on the then Polish southwest side of the city.

The last time I had been in Chicago, I was still in college. I had come to attend my cousin Cindy's big beer-hall wedding. I still had vivid images of that time. Tradition demanded that Cindy, as the bride, was supposed to dance the polka with every man at the event, while the other guests threw money onto the dance floor. Once the bride became exhausted, young women at the party, including myself, were to step in to take her place. When *we* no longer could stand up, the aunts took over. This ritual went on for hours in Chicago, but in Hastings, Pennsylvania, at my grandmother's tavern, the wedding would have been an even more protracted affair. There, although the bride and groom might leave for their honeymoon on the first night (perhaps going to stay in a hotel in another small town like Barnesboro), the rest of the family and friends would continue the party, sometimes for days, until the food that the guests themselves had brought was gone.

When I walked into the beer hall and saw my Polish relatives for the first time in years, those with whom I had spent many glorious summers, I began to cry so uncontrollably that my uncle Lou, who was also in tears, declared, "She's really Polish. She knows how to cry." Because of this visit and others during my childhood, I had some sense of Polish, working-class, Chicago life, but that was all I knew about the city when I moved there to work on the paper.

The *In These Times* offices were located on Milwaukee Avenue, right across from The Bratislava, the best Slovakian restaurant in Chicago at that time. The area was Wicker Park, a then predominantly Ukrainian/Polish/ Puerto Rican neighborhood. When I went to buy donuts for the office at the Alliance Bakery on Division Street, a famous Polish destination, the woman behind the counter began speaking to me in Polish. I asked her how she knew I was Polish and she said that she recognized it in the bone structure of my face. After years in California, where Eastern European origins were not noted or significant, it was at first almost quaint to recognize my identity again in such terms. But, of course, Chicago at that time had the largest Polish population outside Warsaw. In Chicago, ethnic divisions also could be hostile. During the 1960s, Mayor Richard J. Daley had kept ethnic and racial groups deliberately separated, so they would not come together to challenge his hold on city politics. Chicago was thus delineated by north and south, east and west, Black and White, Mexican, Ukrainian, Puerto Rican, Italian, and so forth. Daley knew it was easy to manage whole populations if they were unable to unite and were geographically divided into ethnic and racial neighborhoods, then pitted against each other for resources. He created powerful divisions and mistrust among populations, more extreme than anything I had ever witnessed in New York City where there was plenty of racism but where it was mostly impossible not to intermingle in the public sphere; in New York, class might then have been, and might still be today, even more divisive than race.

One day, a very striking young man came into our office. He was tall and lean, with coffee-colored skin and angular features. He was wearing torn jeans, a white button-down shirt, a black vintage vest, and a fedora (one of the few men I ever met who could wear one well). I was immediately intrigued by the juxtaposition of his cool, urban style and his shy demeanor. Star was a jazz musician, composer, and sound artist who had heard about *In These Times* and wanted to check it and us out. He also had a concert coming up that he hoped we would publicize for him. Over the course of the next weeks, he started regularly visiting me at the office. Soon he and I were having lunch together at the Mexican restaurant down the street, and in the evenings, I was going go hear him play at various clubs on the North Side.

His father was Black and his mother was White. Like other men I became involved with in those days, his creative, bohemian world was strikingly different from my own political, academic one. He drove a cab to make enough money to live on while he composed music and played gigs with his ever-changing band. His friends and associates were street musicians, photographers, poets, artists—all living on the margins of Chicago's art scene. Some were already famous among the cognoscenti and later were destined to become even more so, like the incomparable composer, band leader, and visionary Sun Ra. But most of the artists I met through him or those whose concerts we attended together, were struggling to be heard and seen—playing for money on Chicago's "L" train platforms or trying to "sit in" at clubs, joining sets wherever they could, and sometimes giving private music lessons on the side.

It was fascinating to be with someone who was self-taught both as a pianist and as a composer. He had not attended college and instead launched himself into a life committed to creativity and the avant-garde. He seemed fearless in his willingness to try new forms without hesitation. He wrote original stage adaptations of American classics such as Herman Melville's novella *Benito Cereno* (very impressive to me as a student of 19th century American literature). He tried his hand at sonnets, composed duets for bassoon and "L" train, read voraciously, and had immersed himself in whole bodies of knowledge about urban life, photography, film, and music that I had never encountered. As a result, I, who knew a bit about jazz from my early years frequenting New York City clubs, not only rediscovered that original passion but also added new players to my roster: Bill Evans, Rahsaan Roland Kirk, Bud Powell, Sony Stitt, Art Tatum, McCoy

Tyner, Ben Webster and Mary Lou Williams. For a short time, I even tried to play the saxophone. I learned a great deal about creative freedom from Star—all of which became very useful to me in my later work as a writer, professor, and dean of art schools.

Star was an artist, not only because he wrote texts, played music and composed, but because he approached these disciplines with confidence and curiosity—never daunted by a sense that he lacked "expertise." I realized then that there could be joy in daring to work in such ways and that ideas could take multiple forms. I also came to understand that this experimental approach to creating new work was probably what I had come to Chicago to find.

I left the newspaper after a year, recognizing that, as much as I admired journalism and my colleagues, that form of writing and the lifestyle that came with it was not necessarily the best for me. Other writers were more adept at producing work quickly and briefly. I had a different disposition and knew I needed to return to reading books and thinking more slowly. I had spent the past year at *In These Times* reading nothing but newspapers and magazines, ingesting information, racing to keep up with the events of the present moment. But my experience at the paper also had encouraged me to study photography seriously. I bought an old Rolleiflex 2 1/4-in. camera, turned my kitchen into a darkroom, and started developing negatives into prints. I also began to write and publish small essays in various publications. And, most significant, I began imagining my first book, which, some years later would become *The Invisible Drama: Women and the Anxiety of Change*. I had learned how to think beyond the university and to see what it meant to move from one creative endeavor to another while trying to reach larger, diverse, more popular audiences—and what it felt like not to worry about audience at all. I gained assurance in all of this from proximity to those whose confidence about actualizing ideas seemed boundless, those who did not wait for others to affirm their work and who, in fact, did not really expect (although of course they hoped) that they would be lauded by contemporary culture. Nonetheless, these artists continued making work, although at times they were frustrated by the odd jobs they had to accept in order to pay the rent.

Star and I took a trip together to San Diego. I wanted to show him where I had lived for the previous years and introduce him to my former teacher, Herbert Marcuse, and his wife, the philosopher and activist, Ricky Sherover Marcuse. We all met at the house of another friend who had a grand piano so that Star could play for everyone. It was a great and nervous moment for us both. I knew that Herbert had conventional notions of what art should be and was not surprised when he was confused that my boyfriend called his compositions "jazz," appropriating a category that Herbert assumed would fulfill certain traditional expectations. Star performed his versions of classics such as "Take the A Train," "Round Midnight," "A Love Supreme," and so forth. So, although Herbert was disappointed that he did not recognize these versions, I also could tell that he liked Star a lot and found him intelligent. In his resonant voice, Marcuse exclaimed, "But he is so young, and I am so OLD."

For all the intensity of this romantic connection to Star and its benefits to me as a writer and thinker, I never imagined that our relationship would last. I was not looking for a life partner at that time and, I believed, neither was he. I already had been crushed and psychically undone by the end of my very deep connection to Michael. I could not ever imagine living through such a devastating upheaval again. And I knew intuitively that I had lives left to live with others before I would find the person to finally commit myself to, if ever I did. I imagined Star had similar thoughts. Even though I understood that I was passing through his life, as he was passing through mine, the relationship was very meaningful. Immersing myself in Chicago with someone so rooted in the city, who understood its particularity and was comfortable on the edges of multiple art worlds, opened up so many possibilities for the future of my own thinking and the work that it would lead me to. I surely was not worrying about what was to come next, until I was forced to.

THE RUPTURE

Since the painful end of my relationship with Michael, I had not brought any boyfriends home to meet my parents, nor had I discussed my personal relationships with them. During the aftermath of that breakup, my parents had not known what to say to me or how to offer advice. Their silence made me feel even more alone, so I had not tried to discuss such things with them again, nor had they asked. As a result, they knew very little about the men in my life. And I was aware that, because he was of mixed race, Star would be particularly difficult, if not impossible, for my father to accept. But I was in Chicago and they were in Brooklyn. We usually did not talk about who I was dating, therefore I simply did not tell them about him, as I had not told them about earlier, passing relationships.

My parents, surprisingly, had never pressured me about marriage. How could they when they had spent ten years together before getting married and, once they did, had hidden the fact from both families? I believed my parents' attitudes about marriage were not conventional. When my mother was quite old and living in Florida, she and I were sitting around the pool one morning with her octogenarian friends—all women and one man named Saul. When Saul asked why I was not married and then insisted that I should be, the entire group of women, including my mother, shouted at this poor guy, almost in unison: "Why would she get married? There is no reason." This attitude about marriage is more or less how my parents had always acted, although I knew that they, especially my father, would have loved to have grandchildren.

But during my first year in Chicago, on one of my weekly Sunday phone calls to Brooklyn, my father said that he had had a dream the night before. In the dream, I had a Black boyfriend. I held my breath. "Is it true?" he demanded. "Do you?" I was shocked that he would intuit such a thing—my mother, her family, and I were the mystical ones, not my father—and I was even more shocked that he would confront me so directly with something that had appeared to him in a dream. But even knowing what might come next, I could not lie. How much easier it would have been had I not told the truth. But, of course, I said, "Yes, it is true. I have started going out with an interesting musician-composer." And then, sick to heart even then for doing so, I added, "But he's actually only half Black. His father is Black and his mother is White." How sullied I immediately felt, adding that clause to my response, trying to appease my tyrannically racist father. But I was caught off guard and was desperate to move away from the topic.

I tried to tell George who Star was, what he did, why I was with him, but of course none of that mattered to him in the least. I already knew enough about my father to understand that no rational conversation could possibly follow: the argument was about race and nothing more and as such was illogical and nonnegotiable. But his response was even more bizarre than anything I could have imagined: "I knew it," he said. "You'll marry this man and have children with him. I will have nothing to do with it." Then, for the first time in our lives together, he hung up on me. Shocked, I called right back and spoke to my mother. She was equally mortified by what had happened. Even when we had fought in the past, I was the one who walked out of the room—and also the one who came back days later as if nothing had occurred. But this was different. Because we were not physically together, I could not mediate what had happened with my presence. I tried to explain to my mother that this relationship was new, it was not a marriage, it was not going to be a marriage, and that my father had gone too far in responding in such an overtly hateful, racist way. But even as I was attempting to explain that my father had thrust me into an impossible situation, I knew that she could not help me and that, in fact, she too would suffer as a result. I also knew that I was terrified of losing George.

Because I am an only child, my parents had always been my entire close family. At this moment, there were no siblings to call, no aunts or uncles still alive whom I could reach out to. No one was close enough to me to discuss with them what had just occurred— no one who understood the history of George's behavior in relationship to me, men, and race. There was no one who could help me negotiate with him. That phone call with my father and its consequence was the beginning of a devastating rupture, of my disownment by the father whose love I had believed was unconditional. Although we had fought over similar issues many times, I never imagined that he would cut me out of his heart. Now, unwittingly and involuntarily, I had unleashed something so ugly, primordial, and dark in him that he, going against his own love for me, was willing to exile his only child, his adored daughter, from his life, forever.

My choices of men never were designed to provoke him or anyone else. I was not rejecting familial values. I was not rebellious. I simply was determined to follow my own path, to experience the world in its complexity, to live intensely, to learn from whomever I could, to love whomever I was drawn to. My father's rage, need to control me, his fear and anxiety about my life made no sense to me. But I loved him nonetheless and understood that his reactions had deep roots in his own childhood, in racist attitudes he had grown up with in Brooklyn, and in his business dealings, often in neglected neighborhoods where crime was rampant. He had been held up at gunpoint more than once. For my father, who had little comprehension of the historical and socioeconomic roots of what he was experiencing or, in truth, any desire to analyze them, it all had to do with his belief that Blacks and other people of color were "taking over New York." He saw all disruptions to the city and its safety through the lens of race. At some deep level, in his unconscious and maybe even his conscious mind, he believed I had aligned myself with the enemy. And in doing so, I had betrayed him. Given the laws of the street that George lived by, you were either with him or against him. Now, in his perception, I was most assuredly against him, and his response was to disown me.

I do not know how I survived this period. I am sure I must have spoken to Star about it when it first occurred because we so often discussed racism in Chicago. He lived on the North Side of the city, which was and still is predominantly White and Hispanic, therefore the police stopped him regularly. They searched him without reason, asked for his ID without explanation—something that did not happen to young white men in Chicago, only to those men who, the cops thought, were not "supposed to be" where they were. I knew my father's behavior would not be new or surprising to Star. His White mother's family had also rejected her when she married his father. But I was now completely ashamed of my family and of my father's crudeness, and I was even more ashamed to admit the degree to which it was ripping me apart.

I wrote letters to my father, but he did not respond. I called, but he refused to speak to me. I talked to my mother and tried to make her understand, but I soon realized that she, once again, was caught between us, as she often had been when my father and I fought about the men I was dating or those who called the house when I was in high school. I knew she would be unable to change George's attitudes about race. She said that my father was suffering but did not want to communicate with me. I cried uncontrollably. I found a therapist. I went to New

York City but did not stay with them and could not even visit my parents because my father had told my mother he would refuse to see me.

Once when I was in New York, staying at my friend Ruby's apartment, my parents were having dinner with their friends in Chinatown, as they did each Sunday. My mother asked me if I wanted to join them. I was only in town for a few days, but of course I wanted to see them, desperately. I was extremely nervous about going, but I trusted my father would not make a scene in front of their closest friends, whom I suspected might not have heard a word about any of this. I took the subway and met them on Mulberry Street. When I arrived at the restaurant, there were about ten of them all around a big table. Everyone was very happy to see me, but as I had feared, my father did not get up to greet me and would barely look at me. My mother, taking her cue from him, acted the same. I am sure their friends took note of this behavior, but they said nothing. George focused his attention on everyone else—and particularly on the daughter of a friend of ours, some years younger than I, whom we had known since she was a child. That evening she became the one who mattered. She clearly was flattered that he was lavishing so much interest and attention on her and she was also perhaps confused by this excess, surely unaware of why he was being so cold to me, as if I were an acquaintance he saw from time to time—the daughter of a remote friend, perhaps—and she was his actual daughter. This message could not have been clearer; he had successfully communicated to me that I no longer had any importance to him. I could be replaced. George always knew how to stage a theatrical event.

But as painful as this encounter was, I vowed I would not allow my father to erase me from his life. I was determined to find my way back into the fold, not because I wanted his approval to carry on with my life—I was doing that anyway—but because my greatest terror, far beyond being ostracized, was that he would die before we were reconciled. I knew myself well enough to understand that I could not live with that eternal pain.

THE LETTERS

My father wrote letters. There is an entire box of V-mail—Victory Mail, photocopied by the government— that he sent to my mother during the war and which she saved in a carved, wooden box with a labyrinthine pattern burnt into the lid, a gift he had brought back for her from North Africa. The letters, with a great deal redacted that might have revealed geographic locations of troops, are filled with love for my mother—expressions of how much he missed and adored her, how devoted he was to their life together.

After I was no longer living at home, my father also had written beautiful birthday cards to me, expressing his love, always with a check enclosed. When, after I had an academic success, I mentioned to my mother that my father had not said he was proud of me, I then received a letter extolling my achievements and communicating his deep affection—how moved I was by that letter at the time. As he often repeated to me, "Everything I do is for you. Every dollar I earn is for you." But now I had to learn that there were conditions to such devotion.

Letters from George continued to arrive, but they were dipped in poison. I soon dreaded seeing his bold, large, florid handwriting, not unlike my own, on any envelope. Cards arrived for Jewish New Year's, embossed with gold Hebrew letters and Jewish stars with my father's words added to the bottom: "I hope you enjoy your New Year, with your n—." Each effort to harm me, each act of cruelty toward me was a shock. I tried to imagine what it took for him to plan to destroy me and humiliate himself with such words. Had he gone to a store specifically to buy a card to send to me for the New Year? Had he chosen this one with the intention of adding that sentiment? My Catholic mother did not usually send Jewish New Year's cards, so I doubted she already had a box of them in a drawer. He must have deliberately gone out to find one. Or perhaps he had some such cards in one of his stores? I tried to reconstruct how consciously he was playing out this behavior. For me, it was as if my adored father was now possessed.

The letters were little time bombs. I almost dropped them as I opened the envelope, and I often had to sit down to read them, losing control of my legs. I thought of the poisoned robe and coronet that Medea sends to Jason's bride-to-be, his new queen who would usurp Medea as his wife. The robe was supposedly an offering, a gesture of acceptance by the rejected Medea of her fate and of Jason's choice to aggrandize himself with a new wife. What can be more brutal than a supposed gift that is designed to murder the recipient? Medea's gifts are lethal. When the bride puts them on, they kill her and then her father, King Creon, who tries to save her, instead, also dies in flames. What could be worse than birthday cards that damn a once-beloved daughter to hell? What could be crueler than to be spit on by your beloved father? Who was this person sending poison missives to me now with such devastatingly racist messages? I was shocked at what he had become.

For my entire adult life, I called my parents every Sunday, holiday (Jewish and Catholic), birthday (theirs and mine), Mother's Day, and Father's Day. There were now no longer any phone calls. But a year or so into this nightmare, on Father's Day—when, of course, I did not dare call but had sent a card—my mother phoned to say that my father wanted to speak to me. Could I please hold while she put him on the line? I immediately began to shake. Before I could say a word and without any greeting, he said, "You are a "n— lover and no longer my daughter." Did my mother understand his intentions when she said he wanted to talk to me? Did she set me up for this latest poisoned dagger? I don't think so. She was again caught in the crossfire. All I could do was cry on the other end until he hung up. There would be no conversation, my father was bound like William Blake's Urizen, "in chains of the mind locked up." A few days later, my mother called again. "George has had a heart attack. Do not come." If some members of the family had heard about the rupture between us, they now were probably blaming me for this cataclysmic event. My life as I was living it, his rage and ugliness in response, as well as his already fragile health were probably the reasons his heart had broken apart. He did not die, and at least for this I was grateful.

Months later, I was again staying with Ruby in the East Village when my mother left a message on Ruby's answering machine: "Carol, your father is in Maimonides hospital again. You should try to come." The hospital is in Brooklyn, and in the mid-1980s it was difficult to get a cab to Brooklyn from the East Village in Manhattan. No cabdriver wanted to go out into the boroughs and not have a fare back. At that time, drivers would ask where you were going before letting you get into the cab, and if they didn't like your response, they simply muttered some excuse and drove away. I practically needed to lay down in the middle of Third Avenue to get a cab. I then had to beg the driver, tell him the almost truth, and hope he would relent: "My father is dying," I said. "Will you take me to Maimonides hospital? I will pay you double for the ride."

When I got to the hospital, my father was hooked up to oxygen, but he was sitting up and talking. His doctor had just left. He had blood clots in his lungs. The doctor, who liked my father a great deal and with whom my father had a terrific rapport, had simply said, "George, if you do not stop smoking, I will no longer be your doctor. You are killing yourself."

After this experience, my father did stop smoking, although he had smoked for his entire life. But he had already ruined his lungs, heart, and kidneys as well and had had several near-death experiences. Years later, when recounting this event to others, my father left out the most important elements: "I just decided to quit smoking one day, and I did," he would say, never mentioning that he had almost died and that the doctor had told him there was no chance for survival if he did not quit.

But that day, when I sat on the edge of George's hospital bed, he did not object. Still, nothing between us had really changed.

THE PRODIGAL DAUGHTER

I cannot remember how I functioned during those five years when George and I did not speak, and yet I did. I taught at the School of the Art Institute of Chicago. I worked on my first book. I tried to have a life and a romance. But, of course, the ongoing distress of being severed from my family seeped into my personal relationships, darkening even the most enjoyable moments.

After the fourth year, my mother came to visit her

brother Antoine and my aunt Emma, who lived in Chicago. She, of course, did not stay with me, but she asked to see me and to meet my boyfriend. This request was a big gesture, but I suspected the visit was a reconnaissance mission orchestrated by my father. I thought about how best to present my Chicago life to her, so I asked if I could bring her to Star's studio where he could play for her. She agreed and, on that day, she asked my uncle to drop her in the neighborhood where we lived, which, at that time, was somewhat sketchy. My boyfriend's studio was on the North Side in Lincoln Park and off a small alley. It probably looked less safe to her than it actually was, but she did not comment on any of this. Once inside the studio, my mother, usually so confident, chatty, and engaged with people, was totally guarded and silent. She fidgeted the whole time, opening and closing her purse, arranging and rearranging her chair constantly, and asking for water. Star played beautifully and melodically for her, explaining the intent of the composition as he performed. He was charming.

I could tell that my mother understood how talented and intelligent he was. Star was also a very handsome man, and my mother was always appreciative of that attribute. She had married a handsome man herself. Hoping we would have lunch together with time to talk, I had chosen a nearby Greek restaurant that I thought she might like. But my mother was clearly uncomfortable with us and soon wanted to return to her brother's house.

We, of course, offered to drive her back. In my rattly Volkswagen and because of her unnatural silence, the trip felt interminable. As we got closer to those small working-class homes on the South Side, she asked to be dropped off a block away from my uncle's. At first, I thought she was confused about which bungalow was theirs because they all look so much alike. But my mother, unlike me or my father, had an unfailing sense of direction; even to the end of her life, she knew exactly where she was. I soon realized that she simply did not want us to park too close to her brother's house. She was clearly worried that my aunt, uncle, or their neighbors might see us with Star. He would surely be noticed in that then all-White enclave. When we pulled over to let her out of the car, I got out of the back seat expecting to hug her goodbye, but she quickly grabbed her bag, as if she were rushing to catch a train, and was gone. I am sure my aunt and uncle asked why I had not come in to say hello. What did she tell them? That I was late for an engagement or had work to do or wanted to beat rush hour? What lie had she offered?

Shame. Shame is not guilt. It is an emotion that requires a public context. Shame is what one feels in front of others—for not being good enough, for deviating from the norm, for breaking the rules, for failing to live up to expectations, whether one's own or those of others. Shame on my parents who knew that emotion too well, who had lived it themselves for years, caught as they had been between two religions and fearful of being ostracized by their families as a result. Shame that they refused to see that what they were doing to me was exactly what they had feared their families would do to them, but never did.

My father's Jewish family (especially my Russian grandmother) loved my mother, and my mother's Catholic family (especially my Polish grandmother) loved my father. Still, my parents had waited for a year to make their marriage public out of shame, but once they did, everyone had approved of it. I had tried to remind them of this several times, but in their minds, my situation was so completely different, that their past circumstances were not relevant.

During this time of separation, I wrote a short story called "Ariadne, Ariadne, What's in It for You?" based on the myth of Ariadne and Theseus. In the original myth, Ariadne, daughter of Minos, the King of Crete, fell in love with the warrior Theseus. Theseus had volunteered to save the people of Athens, whom King Minos, as revenge, was sacrificing to a half-human/half-bull, monstrous, creature called the Minotaur. To save Theseus's life, Ariadne offered him the secret to the labyrinth. By unraveling a ball of thread that Ariadne provided, Theseus was able to enter the labyrinth, slay the Minotaur at its center, seize the prized Golden Fleece, and trace his way out again. By aiding Theseus, however, Ariadne had defied her father and was banished from Crete forever. She sailed away with Theseus and his crew, but, according to many versions of the myth, the outcome was not good for her. In one version, Theseus abandons Ariadne on the island of Naxos, where she dies alone in childbirth. In other versions, without a home or a family to return to, she dies of a broken heart.

After spending five years together, I had become very attached to Star and to the creative life we had been living together. But our situations were changing. I had taken a full-time teaching position and was working to meet deadlines to finish my first book. And, as often had happened with previous men in my life, when they sensed that I might move on to a bigger job or a different life than the one we had been living together, they became threatened and left. Such life changes are probably what also provoked Michael, with whom I had lived in California and Montana, to leave when he did. I knew that if I finished my PhD, if I went beyond him in this way, because he had never completed his degree, my presence would become intolerable to him—and so it did. He stayed with me just long enough to see me through the stress of my exams and dissertation. Then it was over.

When I first met Star in Chicago, I was very aware that we were both unanchored in our lives. We were living in marginal worlds that would stabilize for me and for him over time, but not for us together. I also had learned enough about the jazz scene and musicians' lives to understand that I would not do well on the peripheries of that world indefinitely. It had built-in challenges: late-night gigs, the ubiquity of the band in all aspects of his and therefore our life, women groupies who seemed omnipresent and with whom I did not want to compete, and, later, the destructive force of cocaine. But even though a breakup had always seemed inevitable, the event itself was devastating. Star left me for another musician in his band, whom he then, quite abruptly, also married. The shock was not that it happened that way—such behavior was common in the music world—it was that he had chosen someone so unlike me in every way. I felt as if I had not really known the person who would have made that choice, or perhaps that he had not known himself.

This breakup unearthed a deep reaction of abandonment in me. It took time to recover, and after much sadness and disruption, I went on with my life. Yet I never said a word about any of this to my parents. I continued to find ways to visit them in Brooklyn, as awkward and disheartening as my father's lack of response to my presence continued to be. And as had become the norm, I never tried to stay with them when I was in the city. Then completely, unexpectedly, my mother sold the East Flatbush house out from under my father. She saw that the cold New York winters had become intolerable for him. His heart was continuing to fail, his circulation was challenged, and as a result, he was always cold. The warmer Florida weather would help his body and his spirits, she was convinced. And thus, my parents who had no history of even visiting Florida, moved to Tamarac in Broward County near Fort Lauderdale, where my father's sister, my beloved aunt Harriet, lived at the Bermuda Club.

When I went to Florida to see them there for the first time, it was as if we were beginning again. Although I had not said a word about the change in my romantic life, somehow my father must have intuited that I was no longer with Star because he came to pick me up at the airport and, remarkably, acted like his old self toward me for the first time in all these years. Or, perhaps he knew he was not going to live much longer and had decided that being close to me again was essential. I will never really know, but I went along with it, aware that no conversation between us about the past could ever, or probably would ever, be had. Our small family unit was thus able to reconstitute itself, but at its core was an enormous, treacherous abyss, that I would have to navigate forever.

THE SURGERY

By the time my parents moved to Florida, my father was much weakened. In and out of hospitals, as an unwilling patient, he had become irritable. My mother started to feel that he no longer loved her or wanted to be with her because he seemed so unhappy all the time. When she told him this, he got down on his knees and said that she was always and for eternity the love of his life. He just did not feel like himself. The years of chain smoking had destroyed his heart, lungs, and kidneys. At some point the doctors said that his only hope was to have quadruple bypass surgery, but, of course, his body was already damaged, so the operation posed enormous risks.

I was traveling to Florida quite a bit at that time, trying to help my mother and father adjust to his fragility. I flew down from Chicago the night before the operation to be with them. When I arrived at his hospital room, he was eating short ribs. "Ribs?" I exclaimed. "That is the worst imaginable food for you." "But they offered it," he said. "It was on the menu." "You have four clogged arteries," I said. "So?" he replied, "what could the ribs matter now?"

My father seemed very brave that night. They had just been in to shave his chest for the morning operation. He looked clear-eyed and resolved. The odds were in his favor, he had been told. A gambler always, he took his chances. Not afraid of the surgery, he also did not want to continue as he had been—living a life in and out of hospitals, unable to breathe. There really was no choice, he said.

George did not come through that surgery well. After the operation, while he was in the intensive care unit, he hallucinated that he was back in World War II. "Those guys over there are squealers," he said, referring to the other patients sharing the room, some of whom, under heavy sedation, yelled profanities from time to time. He too was very agitated, and yet they could not increase his sedation because that would slow down his heart rate too much. I feared, quite rightly, that the stress of psychically experiencing the war again would cause his ulcer to rupture. Eventually they moved him out of the intensive care unit, but he never really came back to himself.

When my mother and I visited him at the hospital, she often became visibly distraught, because, of course, she knew too well what was happening. One day, while he was hooked up to several machines, including a ventilator, which made it impossible for him to speak, she started to say to him, "I know you thought I never loved you, but I always did. I always will." My father looked very agitated as she spoke. She had loved him, unequivocally. Why would he have doubted that? And he adored her, but although my father's playfulness was always there, I hardly ever saw playfulness between them. Perhaps the vaporous wall that kept me from feeling her love was the same barrier he had encountered—the one that always made me think she wished I were someone else, someone more like her nieces, someone more familiar—not so "other" to her. Perhaps there were moments when she wished the same about my father, but if that were the case, I had never observed it. I could not understand why she was saying these things to him now, but it was not the time to ask. She was upsetting him terribly, and George, on a ventilating machine, was unable to respond. I told her not to talk about such emotional things at this time. I walked her out of my father's hospital room and entrusted her to the ombudsperson, who agreed to sit with her in the family lounge.

I went back to my father's room, sat on the edge of the bed, looking into his very blue and now very troubled eyes, and told him not to worry, that I would always take care of my mother and that I would also take care of myself, that I loved him very much, and always had. I said all this with great composure, never averting my glance. But I saw that my words also were only exacerbating the situation. He looked desperate and trapped in his enforced silence. And yet I knew this moment was my only chance to tell him, perhaps for eternity, that we would be all right, that I would stay close to my mother, always. There was so much more I wanted to say, and so much I knew he wanted to say, but it seemed unfair to continue to try when he was unable to respond. I sat with him for a while holding his hand. I understood the panic in his eyes: we were his to care for, and now he knew he was leaving us. He was not worrying about himself. I could see that he was resigned to what was happening to him. Rather, it was our future, without his presence in it, that frightened him. I reassured him again and again that I would take care of everything. Then, as devastating as it was to do so, I left the room.

The next day, I arrived at the hospital in the late morning. I exited the elevator on his floor, just as they were moving him into surgery, again. I now learned that his ulcer had, in fact, ruptured. Peritonitis had set in—it was all that we had feared. As they rolled him past me, they stopped so I could hold his hand and kiss his cheek. I told him it would be okay, but, even with the ventilator and all the tubes holding him down, he managed to lift his neck and shake his head, "No." He knew what was happening, and so did I. As they wheeled the gurney into the elevator, I leaned against the outside wall of the hallway and slid to the floor, gravity and grief pulling me to the ground. A nurse came to walk me to a chair and brought me a glass of water. I just sobbed. My mother was on another floor signing papers. Thankfully, she had not witnessed any of this.

After that last surgery, George never regained consciousness. Unable to let him go, my mother and I agreed to put him on dialysis. Unable to accept what we knew, that he would not have wanted any of this, we told ourselves that we had to give him a chance. Cowards. The night they called to tell my mother that he might not make it, I was back in Chicago to work for a few days. My mother had asked them not to call her in the middle of the night, no matter what. She was afraid to be told that he was gone while she was alone.

I learned so much from how my father died in that hospital. I knew then that I would not allow my mother to be alone at the very end. I would be there wherever she was, whenever it happened, and, if possible, she would not be hooked up to machines. She would die in her bed, in her home, as her mother and her mother's mother had done, knowing that she was loved until her last breath. But, as illusory as our reconciliation might have been, I was grateful, oh so grateful, that my father and I were at least able to be together at the end.

We brought my father's body back to Brooklyn to be

buried. All his friends— including the Napolis— and our remaining relatives, came to the funeral home on Coney Island Avenue. I refused to let the rabbi make up platitudes about my father, so I wrote something and read it at the service, telling those in attendance how much he would have loved to see them all, how he missed them while living in Florida. And were he present, this would have been his time to say how he actually hated Florida, how impoverished and corrupt it seemed to him, how there were no good Chinese restaurants, and how you had to pay more for a car if you bought it with cash.

I can no longer even remember the details of the burial—only that I had a horrific headache and nothing could abate it for days. Like Athena, who emerged from the brow of Zeus, I had given my father a terrible pain in his head, and with his departure, he had given it right back to me. I spent the first weeks after my father's death imagining my right arm raised straight up to the sky, stretching my fingers like Michelangelo's Adam to reach my father's hand, to make a connection between the physical and the ephemeral on whatever plane he might now inhabit.

Some months after George died, my first book came out—*The Invisible Drama: Women and the Anxiety of Change*. It gained a large popular audience, and I was deeply saddened that my father did not get to see this success. The publisher had arranged a book tour with radio, television, and speaking engagements across the country. In truth, most of these promotional events were quite bizarre. Male interviewers who had not read the book asked me right before we went on the air what questions they should pose; female talk-show hosts, during the break, asked for tips on how to alleviate their own anxiety; discussions of "rising hemlines for the fall" aired before my appearance and performing Dalmatians right after it. What I had hoped would be serious discussions about the state of women's psychological health in the United States became ridiculous and superficial media segments. But I learned a great deal from the experience—enough to know that I probably did not ever want to write a "popular" book again.

I had been working on *The Invisible Drama* for five years, and, in a sense, I was already beyond it when it finally came out. I certainly never imagined the attention that would surround it when it launched, but throughout, I was mourning my father. It took everything I could manage simply to get dressed each day. I was in deep grief, a grief I did not want to interrupt with these events. Loss was all I had left of him. And yet, there was only a small window within which to maximize these invitations to publicize the book; I had no choice. But the juxtaposition of my internal, fragmented state and this public demand for me to be coherent, to be "on," and to have answers for unanswerable questions about individual anxiety, was a tension I could not mediate. After a talk-show appearance in Miami, while visiting my mother in

Tamarac, I suddenly doubled over in pain. I thought the cause might be appendicitis. After a time in the emergency room and many tests later, I learned that it was probably a spastic colon. They gave me some medication to relax the muscles so my body would "forget" to perform that reflex. "What had caused this?" the doctor wanted to know. "My father just died," I told him. I needed to grieve. I wanted to hide. I wanted to be left alone. I probably wanted to die. So much remained unsaid between my father and me, and now it was too late. Being out in the world when I was so shattered, while having to keep this vulnerability from the audiences I was supposed to inspire, had literally made me sick.

I mourned my father for many years—my sorrow was a mix of grief and rage. I am certain I broke his heart. He surely broke mine. I knew I could never agree with his view of the world or with how he sought to impose his fears and prejudices on me. But I also knew that I would never let him go.

UNINHABITABLE TERRAIN

During the years when my father would not speak to me, I also had little contact with my mother. She was so opaque when we did see each other that we never could talk about what had happened among the three of us. I sensed that she did not know how to help me or how to help George move beyond himself to allow me back into his heart. But if my father was willing to lose his beloved daughter, then really what could she do? Or was she simply unable to navigate the terrain between his will and mine, something that always had been difficult for her? Did she stand up for me in private but not in public? Could it be that she was as fearful and racist as my father? We never talked about these things, even though she outlived him by more than twenty years.

The tension between my mother and me—how to unravel that? I felt I would never and could never live up to her beauty or her goodness, which friends, her family, and my father's family all praised. She was incredibly kind and caring toward my Jewish grandparents and also always generous with her own family. My mother was a great caretaker when one was ill or needed physical help. She had always been an incredibly attentive mother to me in those ways. She knew how to make people feel secure when they felt physically precarious. She had boundless confidence in her own ability to heal and in the natural workings of the body to right itself. Yet, for all her openness and attentiveness to others and to me when I was a child, she also had always been emotionally aloof from me. When she did try to mirror me back to myself, as mothers need to do for their children, it was often to focus on my imperfections. When I was a child, she often told me that she thought I was selfish and unable to share with others, as she had had to learn to do growing up in her large, very poor family.

Some of this behavior had origins in the times in which she lived. Hers was not the most self-aware or self-reflective generation, especially among peasant immigrant families like hers. But it was also just not in her nature to praise me in any way or to tell me that she loved me—and yet, of course, I knew that she did. There was also the problem of her narcissism, for which I have never blamed her and still do not. My mother just could not step outside herself long enough to make room for me psychically; perhaps having a child had simply taken up too much space in her consciousness, although I know that, had she physically been able, she would have had many children. Perhaps having more children would have diffused the intense intimacy of raising just one, enough to make being a parent emotionally tolerable for her. When I was young, I often would catch my mother staring at me. At those times, I always imagined that she was thinking the worst about how I looked, what I had become, how alien I seemed to her. I often felt as if she were standing apart, judging me. In such an imagined evaluation of my worth, I always came up short. Remarkably, given my confidence in other areas, I was afraid to ask her what she was actually thinking and what, if anything, she was trying to discern. Perhaps I already knew that she herself did not know why she stared at me, or maybe she was oblivious to the fact that she did.

When my mother was very old and no longer able to prepare our dinners, she finally allowed me to take charge of her kitchen when I visited her in Florida. While I was cooking, she often would sit at the dining room table holding her head in her hands—as if she were contemplating the worn, plastic lace tablecloth she liked to use—humming softly. At such moments, when she seemed to have retreated inside herself, I wondered if there might be something she hoped to tell me and could not? Did she finally want to say she regretted the catastrophe that had occurred in our family, or to say that she too had suffered because I had lost my father (and had lost her as well) for many years? Was she sorry that she did not help me more to resolve matters with George? I never blamed her for what could have seemed cowardice in the face of my father's rage. She had always been a courageous person. But she did not know how to choose between George and me, how to face down that extreme darkness and cruelty that had descended on him and then on us. But many years after her death, and only in a dream, did she say these words to me: "I'm sorry. I'm sorry. I'm sorry, honey." I took this to mean: "I am sorry I was unable to show you all the love I had for you. I am sorry for the wall that kept me from you. I know it damaged you. I know it made you fearful in life. I had never intended that." But those are my explanatory words, not hers. Hers were simple, and I was grateful for them. But by that time, she was speaking to me from another dimension.

After the tensions had inexplicably subsided with my father, enough for me to visit them in Florida with some semblance of normalcy, we finally were able to navigate each other again in the presence of others. I was then with them at the home of their good friends Charlotte and Sonny when their son Alex was also visiting. I had known him since we were children and I was aware that for more than a decade Alex had been ostracized by his family for joining a religious cult, similar to the Hari Krishnas. When Alex and I were alone on his parents' screen porch, he referenced those lonely years during which his family would not speak to him. A bit sarcastically, he said to me, "You wouldn't know about such things, exemplary daughter that you are, always praised by your family." His remarks truly shocked me. "Had you never heard about the five years when my father did not speak to me?" I asked. "Had you not heard that I had a boyfriend George violently disapproved of and that he disowned me and had a heart attack for which I probably was to blame?" Stunned, he answered, "No, never a word about any of that." In the public perception, the earthquake in my life, which had destroyed all habitable terrain between my family and me, for a long time, simply had not occurred.

When I began writing this book, cautiously attempting to lance this abscess again, the poison finally began to drain. Then I had a powerful dream in which my father was being very cruel toward me. Suddenly I became terrified of him. It was as if the person I had known disappeared and, just as in a horror movie when the demonic inhabits the familiar, darkness and silence took over. In the dream, I was experiencing pure maleficence—the complete absence of love. Once again, I thought of Blake's *Book of Urizen*: "This abominable void / This soul-shudd'ring vacuum." At the moment when I came closest to tumbling into the abyss that my father had created, which surely would have annihilated me forever, I began screaming for my mother, like a frightened child, desperate: "Mom. Mom, save me from him." Save me from this man I had so loved and thought had so loved me. But in the dream, she never did. Finally, it was my own strong, loud, and terrified voice that woke me up, sparing me the rest.

Years after George died and the loneliness and missing him had settled into my bones like a permanent, damp, chill, I had his auctioneer banner mounted and framed. I hung it among the art in my Chicago house. This roughly cut, large, hand-painted square, with black letters on white arched canvas strips, floated perfectly in an ebony frame—a bit extravagant, put together by an artist friend for me. It was all I possessed from my father's world and that time of our life together.

It reads:
G. BECKER
Auctioneer
Sale To-Day
Lic. No.497884

When my mother came to visit me in Chicago, she saw the flag on the wall. I was fearful that she would be unnerved by it and feel the loss of him again. Caught by surprise, not having seen that banner for decades and probably unaware that I even had it, I thought she was about to cry as she fixated on the image in silent contemplation. Eyes closed, she stood in place, pointing. Finally, she opened her eyes, scrambled around in her handbag for a piece of paper, found one, handed it to me, and said, "Write that number down, clearly, so I can see it. That's Georgie's auctioneer ID. I haven't thought about it for years. Now, read the number back to me, slowly, and then again."

I did as she said and then returned the scrap of paper to her. Looking straight at me while lifting her eyebrows, as if she knew a secret that I did not, she folded the paper and put it back into her purse, closing the bag's clasp with one hand. Quiet now, unexpectedly thrust into the past, thoughtful perhaps about this fortuitous discovery, and, both happy and pained to again have something of George's in her possession, she suddenly became animated. "There has to be Lotto or something like that on the streets here," she said with excitement. "How about at that bodega we passed around the corner? Let's go out and play George's number, honey. You just never know. Your father surely had the touch. Maybe we'll get lucky."

EPILOGUE:
THE UNVEILING

There was a long period of uninterrupted mourning after George died. The first year was the hardest. My father and my mother had been together for fifty years. I had never known my mother to be depressed, but now she was. My cousin Eleanor worried for her well-being. I knew my mother would come through it, but she needed time. George appeared to her often and to me as well. She and I exchanged stories about these visitations. She always wanted to know how he looked, what was his demeanor in the dream. Sometimes I saw him sitting straight upright in his padded lounge chair in front of the television, late into the night, feet up, no longer struggling to stay awake because he was fearful that he would drown in his own fluids— pulmonary edema caused by a weak heart. During one of these visits to my mother, he shook her awake to tell her she was snoring. Once he was laughing with her, when, while dreaming she was taking a wide turn on a motorcycle, she fell out of bed.

When I was visiting Glacier National Park with friends that first summer after George's death, I saw him in a dream standing next to my mother while she was ironing. She did not notice him. George was angry with me and said, admonishingly, "When you have a vacation, you should spend it with her." I woke up guilty and crying. A month later, he appeared in a blue suit and white shirt, looking young and handsome. He came to let me know that the daughter of our Brooklyn neighbors was going to have a baby, weeks before any of us had been told.

At first these visits were upsetting to us both. After each, I awoke sobbing, the rupture of loss wracking me for days. Even in the dream itself I would break down. Sensing that his raw presence was too piercing for me, my father started appearing behind the windshield of a car, out of focus, looking as if he were underwater. When I asked him how it was to be gone, he replied, "Each day is hard." His chest was bare, and he was shivering, as he was during those last days in the hospital, in a room with too much air conditioning, surrounded by cold metallic basins and by dialysis and respirator machines. He came to me that first Thanksgiving dressed for dinner, disguised as Marcuse, my former professor. But when I discovered who he actually was and began to cry, he said: "You ask to see me and then when I appear, you fall apart." He was silent for a time after that.

My mother and I dreaded the unveiling—the marker of time in the orthodox tradition, a year after the burial, when the headstone is revealed. Fearful we would collapse in grief at the cemetery, my mother suggested we each bring someone close for support. She hired a car to pick us all up in the East Village at her friend Sarah's apartment building on East Tenth Street.

My mother had paid for a limousine, imagining it would be a large, shiny, black vehicle, with its driver in a peaked cap. But when the "limo" arrived, it was a beat-up Chevy.

The car might have looked good ten years before, but now it was dented so the doors barely opened, the windshield had spider cracks, and there were holes where the ashtrays used to be. The driver was disheveled and dirty, wearing a plaid flannel shirt—without a cap. He had no idea where he was taking us. He had not brought a map, and he did not speak much English, but my mother chattered away at him distractedly, nonetheless. It took twice as long to get to the cemetery because, unable to understand her directions, he got lost—not unlike my father, who never could find New Jersey.

Halfway there, my mother, who had a superior sense of direction but had given up on the driver many miles before, began to hum to herself. *"I could have danced all night, I could have danced all night, I could have spread my wings and done a thousand things. . . ."* She kept turning around to ask if we were hungry, pulling out small plastic bags of figs and dried apples from her pocketbook, all of which smelled of perfume. There were no takers. "We'll go to Veselka's to eat when we get back," she said reassuringly.

As we approached the cemetery, the grass looked burnt, but once we were closer, we realized that the grounds were covered with hundreds of grey, brown geese. They were probably migrating south, and more hovered in the air, darkening the sky—gigantic, ugly, overly confident birds. Perhaps they too had gotten lost, finally forced to land in New Jersey, the only expanse of unpopulated land on their route.

The relatives started to arrive. My aunt Julia, the only aunt left, overly made up and wearing a mink jacket, one leg gone because of diabetes, was wheeled in by her eldest daughter, Elaine. The twin cousins also were there, in high heels and black crepe, middle-aged, each having been married, divorced, and married again. We were now an even smaller unit, just my mother and I—conspicuously alone, braced by our two friends, Sarah and Ruby. No sign of the rabbi. Soon Eleanor began to be concerned. She had made the arrangements months before. "Do rabbis forget such things?" she asked. She went to call.

We were bonded in death, Eleanor and I. A year before, we had together chosen the casket for my father, and then a month later, a similar, plain one for her mother—my aunt Harriet, his sister. We had brought her mother's clothes to the funeral home along with her emerald green eye shadow and black mascara to give to the embalmer. Eleanor had been with my mother and me at the funeral home in Brooklyn when I was unable to recognize my father's body. Because we had transported him back from Florida to be buried in New Jersey, someone had to identify him. The mortician opened the casket and asked me, "Is this your father?" I was certain it was not. "No, this is not my father." The body in the box was so swollen and pale, his features were indistinguishable. They had to call in my mother. "Oh yes, it's George," she said confidently. "Those are his shoes. He's just puffy from the weeks on the ventilator." She then made me place my hand on his rigid chest for good luck.

When Eleanor called the rabbi's home, his wife said he was on his way. Another half hour of worrying until a red, close-to-the-ground Alfa Romeo sports car pulled up. A forty-something guy in a cap got out—his license plate read, "MY TOY." "I'm the rabbi," he announced. "Where is the gravesite?" he asked, completely distracted. We chased after him as he put on a jacket and yarmulka. We all looked at Eleanor. She shrugged, as if to say, "A rabbi is a rabbi. What do you want from me?"

In Jewish practice, you place a small rock on each tombstone when you visit, to mark your remembrance for eternity, to say you were there and have not forgotten. Even knowing this well, I had brought red roses, which had lots of stems and lots of thorns. Not at all the tradition.

While the rabbi was leafing through his Bible, I was counting out the roses, placing each carefully on the nearby graves of those relatives who had most touched my heart. Eleanor was trailing behind me. "Don't put any on Max's grave. The bastard," she warned me. "And forget about Sam, the coward." I touched the engraving on my grandmother's stone and on those of my uncle Hymie and my aunt Harriet—the great loves of my childhood. My grandfather, not so much. Still, roses for them all.

When I turned around, I saw the twins crawling on their knees looking for stones, with small black, patent-leather handbags dangling from their wrists. "Could we have brought our own?" Elaine asked. "Or do you have to find the stones here?" No one seemed to know. The glacier long gone and not likely to return, the ground picked over for generations—how could there be enough stones for all the dead? On some family graves there were huge boulders placed on top of the tombstones—boulders that were probably shipped from Wyoming or someplace out West. I took my cousin Evy's hand. She had been my father's favorite niece. She smelled of perfume, still glamorous at fifty-five, a black lace handkerchief covering her head. She had come prepared—grieving, missing her mother who had died twenty years before.

The rabbi was taking his time. "I need to ask you a few questions," he said. "What was your father like? What did he believe in? What was his work? Would you say he was a loving father? Was he a religious man? Were you close?" Jerk, I thought to myself, now you ask, at the last minute? What would you do if I were to tell you that he was not a good man, an atheist, and a liar? Would you actually get up in front of our family and say, "Today we dedicate the gravestone of a sinner who believed in nothing and refused to provide for his family." But instead, I replied, "Don't even try to capture my father. You'll never get him right, not to these people who knew him so well, not in a few sentences. He was funny, ironic, unpredictable, devoted to my mother, a great storyteller, and a bit wacky at times. He could also be extremely irrational and very cruel. But we adored George. We did not ask you here to tell us about him. Just say the appropriate prayers—read the Kaddish in Hebrew. Keep it short. George hated things like this. And don't ask my mother any questions. She's upset and she's not even Jewish."

Now, with all of us assembled in front of the shrouded stone for the final act, I put my arm through my mother's and noticed for the first time that, although everyone else was in black, she was wearing a favorite navy-blue dress with white trim and a short matching jacket that barely closed over her large bosom. She grabbed my hand, and, like Garbo, began to whisper her song: *"Kiss the boys goodbye. . . ."* The empty plot behind my father's had long been reserved for her, and the one next to hers—well, that is for me.

The rabbi pulled the cloth sheet from the gravestone to reveal my father's name etched in sparkling, gray granite, like all the other tombstones. But at that moment the sky turned dark. The rabbi looked up. We all looked up. There, in formation, eclipsing even the sadness, were the geese—low-flying, massive, ominous, like albatross, finally on their way to somewhere warm. "Damn ducks," I could hear my father say, feigning surprise and annoyance while hoping to distract us from the solemnity. "Damn Ducks. What the hell are they doing here?"

ACKNOWLEDGMENTS

Those friends who encouraged the telling of this tale never wavered in their confidence that I would complete the process. They have inspired me with their steadfastness, brilliance, creativity, curiosity. and love: Sarah Abella, Roberta Albert, Janine Antoni, Ramin Bahrani, Alda Blanco, Marin Blazevic, Gavin Browning, Susanna Coffey, Brad Evans, Stephanie Farquhar, Henry Giroux, Eve Glasberg, Matthew Goulish, Adrian Heathfield, Marianne Hirsch, Lin Hixson, Georgia Kotretsos, Litsa Kourti, Gideon Lester, Jesse Cao Long, Roberta Lynch, Laila Maher, America Martinez, Safwan Masri, Diana Matar, Hisham Matar, Denise Milan, France Morin, Peter Murchie, Joey Orr, Katharina Otto-Bernstein, Alice Quinn, Ruby Rich, Ellen Rosen, Hannah Ruby, Jeff Ruby, Kathryn Sapoznick, Noémie Soloman, Lisa Wainwright, Carole Warshaw, Wendy Woon, Jana Wright, and Kathryn Yatrakis.

My beloved partner from the heartland, Jack Murchie, anchors me to this planet and offers wisdom, optimism, and joy every day.

Deborah Cannarella has been an indispensable editor for every book and essay I have written since we met. She is visionary, meticulous, and forever generous of spirit.

I also have been thrilled to work with the editorial staff of Spuyten Duyvil and especially with t thilleman and Aurelia. They immediately recognized the synchronicities that made this collaboration inevitable, including our connection to the real and imagined borough of Brooklyn—their base of operation, the point of origin for this story, and my primordial home.

George's Daughter is a companion volume to Carol Becker's first memoir/essay, *Losing Helen*.

Becker has also written numerous articles and several collections of essays as well as nonfiction books, including: *The Invisible Drama: Women and the Anxiety of Change; The Subversive Imagination: Artists, Society, and Social Responsibility; Zones of Contention: Essays on Art, Institutions, Gender, and Anxiety; Surpassing the Spectacle: Global Transformations and the Changing Politics of Art; Thinking in Place: Art, Action, and Cultural Production.*

Carol Becker is Professor of the Arts and Dean Emerita of Columbia University School of the Arts. Before arriving at Columbia, she was Professor of Liberal Arts, Dean of Faculty, and Senior Vice President for Academic Affairs at the School of the Art Institute of Chicago. She received her PhD in English and American Literature from the University of California, San Diego. She travels widely, lectures about art, culture, and the place of art in society. Her writing, talks, and interviews can be found at caroldbecker.com.

Becker's third memoir/essay, in progress, will focus on her time in California from 1968 to 1978, a decade of revolutionary ideas and actions that continue to transform the world.